It Is ALL Right

ISABEL M. HICKEY

ISBN: 9798668956944

Editor and Publisher: Amy Shapiro (aka Shapiro-Kaznocha) of New Age Sages
Printed in the United States of America via Kindle Direct Publishing

Cover Art by Isabel Hickey.

Original copyright by Isabel Hickey of Fellowship House Bookshop in 1976. The rights passed to Helen Hickey of New Pathways in 1980, and to Donald Hickey in 2005. In its 10th printing, Donald transferred the publishing rights to Amy Shapiro of New Age Sages in 2020 to make this new edition of It Is ALL Right accessible to readers online.

INTRODUCTION

This book goes forth with the prayer that it will bring healing, hope and understanding to my brothers and sisters everywhere. It is written from my heart to yours. The title for it came a few weeks before the book was finished. In that in-between time — between sleeping and waking — I heard a beautiful voice say: "IT is ALL right. It IS all right. IT IS ALL RIGHT." With those words came the consciousness of its truth; no matter what happens in the world of appearance IT IS ALL RIGHT. Right for that moment in time and space — right for the growth of the individual concerned. We ARE vibratorily connected to everything that happens to us. I have found that the reiteration of this sentence changes the feelings in the little self we call the subconscious and changes the consciousness of the outer self. It IS all right.

So let it be.

This book is dedicated to Helen Kay. Hickey, a disciple of light, who chose to come through me as my daughter. Her sustaining help, not only with this book, but in my life has made the journey of life worthwhile.

CHANGERS

PROLOGUE

THE FOOL

Once upon an infinity that had nothing to do with time and space there was a Fool. He danced in a sunlight that never grew dim and was protected by a Father and Mother of Infinite Love. He was forever young and had never known any sorrow or pain. He *was* and had been when the morning stars sang together before they took their places in the meadows of heaven. Everything was beautiful. Perfect harmony, perfect love, perfect everything; but the Fool didn't think so. In fact, he hadn't started to think; but he "knew" he wanted to leave Home. He wanted to see what it would be like to be on his own away from his Father's home. So he felt he had to go. He loved his Father and wanted to be close to Him but felt he would be closer if he left. His older brother rebuked him for he knew the Fool didn't know what he was doing. To his brother, who had chosen to stay because his Will was one with the Father's Will, the Fool said: "You decided to stay. You used your free will to do what you wanted. I am going to use mine to do what I want. I have my wand, my wallet, my feather, and my little dog who loves me and will go anywhere I go. What more do I need? How can it not be right? I want to Experience everything there is to experience in the Universe. I go so I can return, bringing back to my Father and Mother the fruits of my experience.

With his jaunty feather waving in the breeze he stepped out and started down the mountain. His eyes were on the far hills and he wasn't looking where he was going. The older brother called "Look out and look down!" But it was already too late. The little dog had tried to warn him by barking at his heels but the Fool — and Fool he was — was so busy looking up he didn't see the abyss at his feet. Over the edge of the precipice he went, tumbling down into the valley below, where he landed in a briar Patch and was knocked unconscious.

The little dog watched in dismay as his master went over the cliff for he knew his master was a Fool but he loved him, so he had to follow wherever his master went. He found his way down the mountain, falling some of the way for it was steep, zigzagging through thickets and brambles until he reached his beloved friend. He barked and barked until the Fool awoke. The Fool was still dazed and not at all sure who he was or how he got there. He felt there was something he should remember but he couldn't recall what it was. He knew that he was going on a journey to seek his fortune and that the little dog was his constant companion who would not be left behind. He really must have knocked himself out for he could not remember where he came from or how he got there; but he knew he wanted to go somewhere, even if he was not sure where he wanted to go.

It was time to get started, so the Fool picked the brambles off and gathered up his wand, his wallet and the rose that he must have brought with him. There were no roses anywhere around the briar patch. He checked to see if his feather was still on his head; it was but it had to be straightened. So straightening it out, he started again.

He found himself in a strange and rather desolate place. The sun was hot along the open road. Seeing a forest in the distance the Fool decided to go in that direction. Night was coming on and perhaps it would be cooler in there. He was not quite awake; the fall into the briar patch had made him dizzy and sleepy. His head ached. He knew there was something he should remember. What was it? Well, he pondered, before journeys end it would come to him. All he "knew" was that he had to keep going. There wasn't much time before night. Strange, that he had never wondered about Time before. He felt it had something to do with this place and space. Oh well, maybe he would find out if he kept going.

Strange how dark the forest was. Darkness was a new experience and it was peculiar. It gave him such a strange sensation. He'd never seen a forest like this one. He had a dim memory of forests that were sun-dappled and of trees there that made beautiful music as they grew, but this forest was dark and misty, and for the first time he felt fear. Even the little dog was acting oddly, for he did not jump up and down and run ahead as he usually did, but stayed close to his master instead.

They were deep in the forest now and the Fool felt very sleepy, so he laid down under a tree. He put his wallet under his head and laid his wand down beside him. His little helper lay at his feet, much more awake than he was. He did not know that the little dog's name was Subby, that it played the part of his Subconscious, his instinctive self. Just as he drifted off and out of his body he was brought back with a jolt. His little friend was barking wildly. A robber was leaning over the Fool trying to get his wallet from under his head. The Fool grabbed his wand and used it to ward off the thief while the little dog bit at his heels. The robber decided it was not worth all the trouble. There probably was not much in the wallet anyway so he took off.

The Fool was wide awake after that experience and, holding his dog in his arms, began to ponder. Why was the wallet so important? He knew it was important, though he didn't know why. His little friend looked up at him and answered him silently. Of course: it contained his values. The Fool didn't know what they were, but they had something to do with his memory and his past experience. Although the wallet belonged to him, he was not supposed to look into it, at least not yet. He knew, without knowing how he knew, that if he looked into the wallet he would get lost in the labyrinth of the past. His way lay straight ahead, not behind. He must go on with his beloved companion wherever the road would lead them. So the Fool hung his wallet on his wand and started out, whistling to his Subby to come along.

They walked out of the forest just as the sun was rising. As the Fool looked at the sunrise, he almost remembered what he had forgotten. He looked down at the dog and realized his helper remembered more than he did. It was as though his little Subby was saying to the Fool: "Why did you have to leave home? We didn't have to do it! Oh, well, let's go." And off they went again, the dog running ahead, and the Fool whistling as they traveled. It was a strange tune that he whistled, and he did not know where it came from or why the words of the tune sang in his brain:

> "No matter where I wander
> No matter where I go
> My father's love goes with me,
> That's all I need to know."

As the sun rose high in the heavens, the Fool and his little dog came to a field of poppies growing in the sunshine. The colors were so beautiful with the sun on them! He didn't remember having seen such colors before. He wanted to linger and enjoy them, but his little dog was trying to tell him something! "Look at their beauty and enjoy it, but leave them there. Don't be drugged by the senses. Even beauty can be a trap. It's hard to find your way out if you're caught in the world of appearance." It would have been fun to linger in the sunshine and forget about the rest of the journey, but his little friend would have none of that nonsense. Subby wanted to be on his way. He would leave the Fool behind if he did not come along. The Fool did not want to be left alone, so on they went through the poppy field and joined the highway again. The Fool's feather was drooping and he felt weary. He began to wonder how long the journey would take, and what lay before him. As he strolled along, he began to wonder why the experience with the robber and the poppy field seemed to be tied together. He had not reached the thinking stage yet, but he sensed and felt that there was a relationship there. Of course! His wallet was the repository of his values. As long as what was in the wallet was intact, his sense of values would take him safely through the danger of being drugged by the senses. Like the poppies, the senses were beautiful in their proper place — but one didn't spend one's life in a poppy field.

The Fool felt good when he reached that conclusion. He knew he had passed one real test. Even his droopy feather perked up, and his little friend seemed happy as he looked up at him. On through the day they wandered, and at sunset they found a place, near a pine tree, to spend the night. It was in a field near a spring where the water was fresh and cool. The Fool did not know what the days ahead of him would bring, but somehow it did not matter at that moment. He had beside him his friend who snuggled up to him as he lay on the moss and watched the stars come out.

He fell asleep, and dreamed he was back Home where all was Peace and Love and Light. He did not know that the dream was real, and that what he called reality was really a dream. One day he would know that he had dreamed a dream of having left His Father's home and gone to a far distant place where he had many adventures and experiences. On that day he would know with all his Being that he had never really left his Father's Home at all. He would wake and know he had been there all the time. Then he would see the dream for what it was. In that day he would know who he was. He would no longer be the simple Fool because he was ignorant an untried, but the Anointed Fool, for he had been through the testing of fire, air, earth and water, and had triumphed.

Morning came and his little friend, his Subby, who always awakened him when he had been instructed to do it, licked his face and was jumping on him. The Fool didn't remember where he had been while his body energized itself, but he felt wonderfully happy.

His sense of adventure was back. The day was going to be exciting, and he figured he had better be on his way.

He and his little dog wandered all day long, stopping to rest when they were tired. For nourishment they ate the berries and fruit that they found along the wayside. As the sun was going down over the distant hills they came to a bridge over a river and saw the town beyond. They stopped on the bridge to rest for a few moments before going on. The town had a wall around it, but there was a big gateway and through it they saw people moving along a street, talking and laughing. The people seemed to be friendly and happy. The fool quickened his steps, for suddenly he realized he had been alone all the way except for his little dog, and companionship would be very welcome. The Fool and his Subby went through the gate and into the town.

Suddenly he felt very uneasy. The air seemed very heavy and thick. He could not understand it. As people turned to look at him they laughed at his weird costume, and instead of talking to him they were talking about him to each other. They appeared to be very important, so the Fool and his little dog decided to act as if they were also very important. But somehow, they could not do it for they knew they were not being themselves. And yet, they knew they would have to playact if they wanted to be accepted by the crowd. If only the people were more friendly! If he took off what he was wearing he would have to take on what they wore. This would include their opinions as well as their clothes. He sensed eyes all around him, and they were not friendly "I" 's. Their negative and prejudiced opinions showed in their faces, thickening the atmosphere and making it sticky.

The Fool and his Subby knew they had to walk through the town and not get caught in the sticky substance. This was the hardest test they had known in their journey so far. They wanted to be accepted. They looked at each other and a look of love passed between them — real love — for it had no end of its own to serve. They had each other.

This gave him the courage to walk through the town and out the other side. At the end of the town, standing on a hill, they saw a hermit waving them on.

A little way from the town they found a running brook singing along in the twilight. They bathed themselves in the brook and felt clean again. All the heaviness was gone. They also felt calm and comforted. Tomorrow was another day to be met when it came. They found a tree that looked so friendly they decided to sleep underneath it. In a few minutes of earth time they were out of the body. They did not come back until the sun awakened them.

It was the fifth day. They woke with a sense of excitement. The little dog jumped up and down, eager to be on the way, for he sensed there was something around the corner that might be fun. Off in the distance around a bend they could hear music. It was a gay and tinkling tune, so they hurried to see from whence it came. Around the bend in the road they found it source; it was a carnival in full swing. Oh! What fun! They saw a merry-go-round going round and round while the music played. Strange. It didn't go anywhere but round and round. Barkers were selling their wares. At one tent dancers were swaying and swinging their torsos, and the barkers were saying there were more wonderful things inside the tent. At another tent the barkers were talking about three-headed babies, midgets and the fattest man in the world. It was all very exciting. Even Subby was running around in circles, he was so excited by the music and the noise and all the activities. It was different from the town. Here the people wooed you and would hypnotize you if you were not careful. They were very clever. With the music playing and all of the noise, one did not have time to wonder what it all meant. The Fool took his little dog and went on the merry-go-round. Perhaps there he could ponder its meaning. Round and round and never going anywhere ... of course! This was the fifth day. This day was trying to tell him something about pleasure and glamour. Though he'd forgotten where he was going and didn't know who he was (at least not yet), he knew he shouldn't linger there or he would not be able to get off the merry-go-round. It was fun, but with a sigh he climbed off and walked away from the excitement and music. He wondered about the dancers, the midgets, the fattest man in the world and the three-headed babies. Were they happy? How did they get stuck in a place like the carnival when there was a great big world outside that should be explored? Well, he had better be on his way.

As usual, the Fool and his dog were very tired by the end of the day. After a sleep that night out in an open field, they were awakened by a skylark singing to the morning sun. It sang with such joy and abandonment. "How strange," felt the Fool, "what a difference between the music at the carnival yesterday and the skylark singing this morning. One seems of the earth, tinkling and like gaudy tinsel; but the bird's song must come from a very high place for it is pure. It reminds me of something, but I cannot remember what. Somewhere, sometime before, I've heard music like this. How I wish I could remember."

As the Fool and his Subby walked along a broad highway they came to a fork in the road. One road went to the right and the other to the left. Which one should they take? The Fool felt confused as he sat on a rock to think. Up to this moment he had been feeling his way along but now he had to *think* in order to make a decision. It was a new experience! He had to get his 'think' box going. He had to oil the gears of his brain. His little dog was lying asleep in the sun. He would not be any help.

The road to the right was smoother and looked as though it led through a town. The road to the left was full of weeds and grass; it was rocky and led uphill. The road to the right looked easier. He hesitated and looking around to ask his friend what he thought, he was nowhere to be found. Subby had gone, and the Fool was truly alone. There was no one to help him make his decision. He looked everywhere for his dog but Subby had deserted him. He did find something, however. It was a sickle, lying in front of him gleaming like a half moon. He realized he could use it to clear the path if he took the left-hand road. Maybe it was a sign! Maybe he should take the path that needed clearing. Maybe it was time he did something that would help someone else. If he cleared the path, someone coming after him would find the going easier.

Beside the road he could see an orchard full of apple trees. People were picking fruit. It was harvest time and they were working hard. He watched them working. They were different from any of the other people he had met on his journey. They were quiet and seemed to enjoy their work. He walked over to the orchard and watched them. They greeted him in a friendly fashion and offered him fruit, but they kept on working. There was a tranquil feeling about them even though they were busy. He wondered if they were peaceful because they were working. These busy people seemed so much more contented than those he had seen in the town or at the carnival. Without saying a word, they were telling him something. The easiest way was not always the best way. And so, picking up the sickle, he started to clear the left-hand road.

It was rough going, for the road was thick with undergrowth and went uphill, but he was determined to clear it. After many hours of hard work, he came to the brow of the hill and saw before him a beautiful valley, and a clear road descending into the valley. It looked inviting but he was so tired from the unaccustomed work that he decided to have a rest before he set off again. Lying down by the side of the road he fell asleep until morning. When he awakened on the seventh day, he knew that the days behind him had each been tests which he had to pass. He had met the tests of the first six signs of the

Zodiac: the descent into matter (Aries); the test of values (Taurus); the test of the senses (Gemini); the test of getting caught in mass consciousness (Cancer); the test of pleasure and glamour (Leo); and the test of service and decision-making Virgo. Now before him lay green pastures and still waters, and the day of rest had come. But this was not the end. It was a new beginning. All this, the Fool realized.

As he walked down into the valley, his dog came running to meet him. What a glad reunion! He had thought his little friend was lost forever. The dog was trying to tell him something. As the Fool listened with his heart, he knew his friend was saying that he had to leave him for the Fool needed to make a decision and a choice without any help from his Subby. The Fool had to use his mind to think things out, for his emotions would keep him from using his reason. So his Subby had left him and gone ahead to wait for him in the valley of rest.

The Fool and his dearer-than-ever little friend had a wonderful day together in the valley. They knew the journey was not over, for on the other side of the valley was a path that climbed the hill beyond, and it would take them where they had to go. They realized, too, that they were going to look for a magician who lived in a castle over the hill. He had something to teach them, and somehow they knew they had been searching for him since the journey began.

When the time came to leave the peaceful valley, the Fool picked up his wallet and wand, straightened out his feather, whistled once more to his friend, and they set off to seek the magician. They had no trouble finding the castle, for the sun had painted every window in gold. They were burning with curiosity. What was the magician like? What was he going to teach them? Did he know *everything*? And how did he learn it? The Fool had so many questions to ask him! Would the magician answer them?

They came to the castle and knocked on the great door that stood ajar. No one answered. Timidly, they pushed it open an entered. They saw a huge hall, and at the end of the hall a large mirror. Nothing else. They walked down the hall and looked in the mirror. In it they saw two figures, but not those of the Fool and his friend, subby. They saw a Magician standing behind a table on which were a wand, a sword, a pentacle and a cup. Beside the Magician stood a High Priestess. Suddenly the Fool realized that *he* was the Magician, and that his real work was just beginning. The little dog would still be his helper in a different form, for without her, the High Priestess, he could not make magic. Magic it would be, in its highest and best sense. He would have other helpers too, for he could do nothing by himself.

So let it be: the training, the work, the teaching, the way, and the "Light that will light the way."

CHAPTER I

THE JOURNEY

Here we are on the earth plane. The Fool, having come down to the physical plane, encasing himself in a garment of flesh, becomes the magician. Let us think of the earth as a planetary school where we have come to learn how to be creators in our own right. We did not want to stay up on the higher planes we chose to come down in order to be co-creators with the Creative Power of the Universe.

So the fiat went forth: "Let us give these rebel angels a planet of their own where they can learn to create. Until they have knowledge of how to create there will be many miscreations. They cannot be allowed to create in the higher dimensions until they learn to create wisely. With them will go two angels. They will call these angels by many different names. One they will call the Angel of Light, and one the Angel of Darkness. For a long time they will not know that both are equal in my sight. One will be called good, and the other will be called by many names: the Devil, Satan, or Saturn. The latter will also be called the Scapegoat, and on him will be placed all the blame for the destructiveness that people will not want to accept as their own creation. There will be only one restriction on the use of their free will. Whenever they use their free will and creative powers, they will be held responsible for their own creations."

Into the law of duality we all came. In the allegory of Adam and Eve it was when we tasted the fruit of the Tree of Knowledge of Good and Evil that we were expelled from Heaven. That state of consciousness in which we do not see anything but good (God) is still there within

1

us. As long as we look only at the world of appearance and see it as double, we do not see the truth. "Let your eye be single and your whole body will be filled with Light." When we can see through the appearance to the reality behind it, we begin to see with the inner "I", the essential Self in every one of us.

At the center of every experience or every person there is stillness and truth. Nature teaches us and exemplifies that truth. At the center of every hurricane, tornado, typhoon or whirlpool is a point of absolute calm and peace. That point is deep within us. Until we still the outer senses and look within we do not know that point is there.

Now we are the Magician. We wanted to "do our own thing," and have our own way, learning from experience how to live and how to love. As the Magician, on the table before us we have the tools with which to work, but the power to use those tools, whether constructively or destructively, comes from above. The Magician brings the life force or energy down from above and uses it in his earthly endeavors.

There is only one Power. It is the life force without which nothing could exist. On the table are the Sword (fire) symbol spirit that will cut away all that hinders us on our journey; and the Wand (air) symbol of the mental faculties through which we learn discrimination. Only in a world of duality could we have choice. Only through making choices do we gain experience. Then there is the Cup (water) which symbolizes the emotions which have to be lifted up and used rightly. The pentacle (earth) represents matter, or the physical plane, the gift of living in an earth body which enables us to have a temple in which the Essential Self dwells. The body provides the house for our being.

These symbols correspond to the four psychological types described by Carl Jung: intuition (fire, spirit), thought (air, mind), feeling (water, emotions) and sensation (earth, the physical senses). These are also the four decks of our playing cards: Spades or Swords are fire, Clubs or Wands are Air, Hearts or Cups are water, and Diamonds or Pentacles are earth. As we become aware, over and over we find the evidences and proof of truth depicted in many ways all around us.

In all schools, education starts on a very simple level, kindergarten or a similar entry level. We start in the lower grades where lessons are concerned primarily with play and learning about others. Then we move on through the succeeding grades. We can stop formal learning at the end of high school or go on to college. At the end of our college years we can get a B.A. or a Ph.D., or whatever degree we choose. That choice is ours. If we fail a grade, we repeat it over again. At times in our learning process and after completing each grade we have a vacation. We withdraw from the physical body bringing with us the essence of all our individual experiences learned up to that time, and we go Home for a rest. After rest and reflection back to the Planetary School we come.

It is the amount of experience we have had in earth bodies and how we have gained it that decides the age of the soul, not the age of the body. When we understand this truth, we do not condemn or judge others. How can we? If I am in the eighth grade and dealing with someone in the fourth grade, I cannot blame him for not having eighth grade knowledge. The fourth grade is where he is. If I live my eighth-grade knowledge and help him through loving him, he will reach the eighth grade sooner. If I call him stupid because he does not know what I know, then I am the one who is really stupid. People do the only thing they can do with the consciousness they have at any moment in time. If they knew better, they would do better. People may know a thing with their minds, but if they don't realize it in their hearts, that thing is not really true for them. "NEVER MIND." We say that phrase all the time, but we never really hear what it says. No one will ever solve the real problems of life with his mind. The solutions lie in the correct use of both the heart and the mind. This truth is not

3

understood on the planet today. That is why the planet is in such a bad state.

The world of appearance is the manifestation of our own consciousness. Nothing is created in the outer world. That world is a reflection of our inner world. Consciousness *is* the only reality. If an architect is going to draw up plans for a building or house, he has to start with an idea in his own consciousness. Then he draws a blueprint. From that blueprint the house is built. He has the freedom to choose the type of house he wants to build. When that house is built it is the manifestation of his own concept, his own idea. Even if the house is destroyed, it can be rebuilt, because the original idea is still within his consciousness.

If in our ignorance, we should build the wrong patterns of thinking, feeling and acting, we still have all the Power we need to destroy our wrong manifestations and rebuild them nearer to our heart's desire. CHANGE is the keyword of the outer world. We can never know any real peace if we depend on the outer world for stability of happiness. It cannot be. The outer world is like a roulette wheel. "Round and round it goes and where it stops nobody knows." At the Center is the only permanence. We can have fun with the roulette wheel. We can enjoy the outer world and learn to play in it. But let's not get stuck in it. If we think that that is all there is, and take it too seriously, we lose all the humor and enthusiasm that should be part of our livingness.

Nature gives us the secret of Life if we look around us. Nature has many moods. There are days of sunshine and days that are dark and cloudy, rainy and stormy. What good would it do the planet if all it ever received was sunshine? It would wilt. What would happy if it never rained to soften the soil and keep the plants from drying out? We can be dried-up intellectuals or bogged-down emotional types if we want, but we don't' *need* to be. We have to find a balance. Andrew

Jackson Davis, one of the greatest seers of the past, gave his staff a formula on which to depend: "In all things keep a balanced mind."

Everyone passes through a lonely. of isolated self-consciousness. If we stay there, we get stuck in the mud of our own egotism. Some stay in it for many lives, from ignorance, thinking wrongly, feeling negatively, acting selfishly. Unwittingly, this is their own choice, for they are not their bodies, their minds or their emotions: they are *spirit*. They create their own hells, as we all have done at one time or another. What they created they can redeem and so can every one of us. We have free will and can choose to sleep in matter as long as we want to. But if we do, we crystallize. Growth stops. Why did Lot's wife turn to a pillar of salt? Because she insisted on looking backwards, instead of going steadily onward. When we live in the past, we do the same thing.

> "So gird on they armour, keep steadily onward,
> Hold they Light that others may see.
> Thy path trodden bravely will leave Light behind it,
> And the road onward leads Homeward to Me."

CHAPTER II

WHY WE ARE WHERE WE ARE

We chose it. We chose where we are from the soul level, not from the personality level. Our spirits, before they came to earth, chose the environment that could best develop the powers required for greater growth. Before we encased ourselves in our threefold vehicles (physical, emotional and mental) we selected our parents. We chose the environment that we needed for the lessons we had to learn as well as the talents we had to develop during this lifetime. Some souls are planted in very trying circumstances with parents who are young in soul and apparently asleep to spiritual things. Sometimes we choose cruel and unloving parents because we have been like them in other lives and are reaping the harvest of wrong choices and wrong actions. For instance, if one is a child born out of wedlock, then in a previous life we were a parent who refused to be responsible for the soul who came through us. In this life we would choose to be born out of wedlock and feel the same pain we inflicted on others in the past. Sometimes we choose these difficult environments, either for growth in some quality that is lacking, or to bring Love and Light into an atmosphere that needs it desperately.

We were allowed the choice to be creators in our own right. We were given the freedom to choose the path we would take. Once we made a choice, we had to abide by the decision we had made. We have to accept the responsibility for the use of our creative powers. If we misuse energy and create wrongly, we must redeem our miscreations.

7

We can create Heaven or Hell by our own actions and reactions. Even on the material level parents are responsible for the children they bring into birth. What of the creations we make through our thinking and our feeling? We are responsible for them too. Having been of a very negative nature in my earlier years it was hard for me to accept that I was bringing my own difficulties on myself. Nevertheless, it was true. I preferred to believe that everything and everyone around me was the reason I was miserable. I was not to blame. If circumstances were only different, I could be different. That is what I thought but it is not true.

My first realization came when the law of reincarnation (rebirth) and the law of the boomerang (karma) were explained to me. If there was no such thing in the universe as a straight line and space is curved, then everything sent forth has to come back to its creator, either for good or ill. If we came bound into this livingness because we had abused the way we used our creative energy in other lifetimes, then God could be a God of Love and I could stop blaming Him, or anyone else, for what was happening to me. I stopped saying, "Why should this happen to me?" I changed it to: "What is there in me that is attracting these circumstances?" When I realized that I had the power to create Hell for myself as well as the power to create Heaven I was on my way. It was difficult because for so long I had built a habit of thinking and feeling negatively, without consideration for my own responsibility in such thinking and feeling.

One day a very beautiful person gave me the way out. Though I knew little of the universal laws, I had faith in her. What a priceless quality that is — to be the kind of individual that instills faith in another. She believed in me when I did not believe in myself. Her words were, "Isabel, for so long you have filled your subconscious self with negative thinking and feeling. These patterns must be changed. I am giving you two sentences. You must say them over and over again to and within yourself. Say them a hundred times a day if necessary. When you say them imagine how you would feel if it were so. This is a secret so few know. If you think a thought long enough it takes you over and you are the thought. It goes to work to outpicture itself in your environment."

These are the sentences that transformed my consciousness, and thereby my life:

"ALL MY WAYS ARE PLEASANT WAYS AND ALL MY PATHS ARE PEACE."

and

"IN QUIETNESS AND CONFIDENCE SHALL BE MY STRENGTH."

Living a life of quiet desperation helped me to say them over and over hundreds of times each day. Slowly and steadily I began to change inside and as a consequence circumstances in the outer world began to change too. I learned we are vibratorily connected to everything that happens to us. There is only one way we can change what is happening to us in the outer world. Change our attitudes our (consciousness) and what is in the world of appearance has to change. The outer world is the world of manifestation, not the creative world. That world lies within us. We all have basic a basic keynote to which we, and the circumstances around us, vibrate. If we change our consciousness, by Cosmic Law one of two things has to happen. Either the person or problem is removed completely (with no harm to the opposing force) or the situation changes so much there is no longer a problem. Because there is a change of keynote to a higher vibratory wavelength the events or persons connected with the old keynote fall away. I have never seen this technique fail if the individual applies the principles inherent within the principles.

Do you remember the story of Jacob and the Angel? Jacob was lame in the hip. Those who know astrology know the hips in the physical body are ruled by Sagittarius, sign of the Higher Self, and also our perception and understanding. Hips give us the power to move forward. Jacob was lame in his understanding. He wrestled all night (the darkness of his own ignorance) with the Angel (his problem) and would not let the Angel go until it blessed him. When he received the blessing (found the good in it) it was morning (light came) and the angel (the problem) departed. Bless your circumstances or people who are giving you difficulties and see for yourself what happens.

We give people or circumstances the only power they have to disturb us or hurt us. If we are depressed or full of fear, we bring forth that which is imaged and expected. The Light is always there but we have to turn on the switch that releases the energy that will conduct the Light. If we go into a dark room, do we find the darkness, or do we turn on the Light? Where is the darkness then? That is why the Master said, "Resist not evil but overcome evil with good." Fighting or resisting increases the difficulties. One thing that happens when we turn on the Light within us is a bit of a shock. We see the dust and dirt, the "pussy willows" in the corners of our characters. We have to go to work to clean up our own house. We see things in ourselves we never knew were there. We have to become conscious of our own flaws and distortions before we are ready to change them. If anyone tried to tell us about them before we were ready to see them, we wouldn't accept them. These circumstances and laws of truth are the same for all individuals. Did unloving criticism ever change any of us? Does a chicken hatch in a cold and frigid incubator? Only warmth (another word for love) creates the climate that will help the chicken grow and expand until the shell around him can no longer contain him. Then his own energy breaks through the shell, and he is in a new and more expanded world. If you try to take off the shell, or release him before it was time, the embryo would die. Is it not the same with individuals?

If we are cold and critical the potential of beauty and lovingness that is in every one of us withers.

If we would only learn to bless the situation that "bugs" us, we would live in a much happier world. One day a woman came to my studio for counseling. After figuring out her astrological blueprint I saw her difficulties lay in her job and her attitudes toward it. Her face was heavily lined. She was tense and nervous. She hated her boss and was ready to walk out on her job. I knew from the cycle she was in that if she did, she would be out of work for a long time. She was in her fifties which would make it more difficult to get work. I saw that she was a person who liked games of chance. She was a Sagittarian. They are known as the gamblers of the zodiac. I asked her to try something before she actually decided to quit. I told her that if the method I suggested did not work within seven days I would then pay her triple what she was paying me that day. She wanted to know what she had to do. I told her she would have to ask God to bless her boss and the job. She was she was to do it the last thing at night, the first thing in the morning, and just before she opened the door of the office. I won't tell you where she said she would see him first! Finally I persuaded her to try the suggested method. She had nothing to lose and had much more to gain than she knew. As she left, I told her I would see her in a week from that day if her job circumstances did not change. The week passed, and I did not see her.

Three months later she walked into my studio with another person. I did not recognize her for she looked ten years younger. After she identified herself, she pointed to the other girl and said to me: "Tell her." I said, "Tell her what?" "Tell her what you told me. It did not take seven days. It only took three. I still have to do all the boss's work, but I do not mind because he's so pleasant. (Note that statement carefully.) Everyone in the office is happier. How did this magic work?" "You got yourself out of the way so that God could work

11

through you to change the situation. You changed your attitude and the circumstances around you had to change. In blessing the boss and the office God's energy had to pour through you and it healed you."

CHAPTER III

GOING GOD'S WAY?

Easy? Whoever said it was? Anything worthwhile and of eternal value has to be earned. The words discipline and disciple go together. Skills of any kind are backed by hours of hard work to develop those skills. Skill in action always looks effortless, but the discipline behind it makes it look that way. It takes repeated practice and prolonged patience in learning to get unhooked from the pull of the outer senses and the world of appearances. We have been caught too long. For so long we have looked outside for what we want, not knowing the outside world is not the world of creation. The outer world is the world of manifestation, where what we have created inside is projected outwardly. We make our own heaven and our own hell. It took thirty years before this realization came to me.

Everything begins on the inside. There is nothing manmade in the outside world that did not begin as an idea in someone's mind. Skyscrapers, houses, washing machines, gas stoves, television sets, brooms, fly swatters, and a trillion other inventions began as ideas in someone's mind. Once the ideas were conceived and brought into manifestation, they could be repeated ad infinitum in the outer world. Could there be wars if the hatred and greed and desire for power did not start in the minds of men? Could our personal world be a shambles if we really knew we had created it and that there is a way to rectify the situation?

Energy *is*. Energy is forever, and is always pure. It is how we use it that determines its effect in the outside world. We are creators. What we create in our minds and our and in our feelings, good or bad, is very important for it if it is projected into our personal world. Imagination — image in — is one of the greatest tools we have at our disposal. When I realized that the Hell I was in was of my own creation, my next thought was that if I had the power to create Hell for myself I had the power to create Heaven. I stopped blaming anyone else for my difficulties. I was where I was because of what I was. I began to work at being a more loving person. Without fully realizing it I had started the spiritual journey. The very first step is to want to be a different kind of person. Then we stop trying to change anyone else and go to work to change ourselves. Most of us have no idea how difficult we are until we really see ourselves as others see us. It is a shock, but until we see it as it is, how can we change?

Giving up self will and letting God's will run your life is not done in one fell swoop, but the desire and willingness to try is the beginning. It is the beginning of the development of one spiritual muscles. And there are many ways to the mountaintop of Spiritual Consciousness. My Initiate Teacher once told me, "You can walk, you can run, you can crawl, you can be pushed. You can choose any road you wish and take as long as you wish on the journey. You can make it easy or difficult for yourself. Like everyone else you are on the way to the mountain top. The end is sure, and sooner or later everyone will arrive at the same place." Brother Phillip taught me that the way was through daily attunement to the High Self and learning to listen to its guidance. Only through the quieting of the mind and the outer senses could we know the higher way. Only a very small part of our total being is focused on the physical level. There is a part of us that has not descended into matter. That is the High Self — the Essential Being — the Divine Spark in every one of us. That self already has all the power, all the love, and all the harmony we can ever use. If we want it we have to withdraw from the outer world in our consciousness and seek it in the stillness deep within each of us.

We do this when we quiet down the threefold personality, the physical, emotional and mental self. It is in the quiet time that we see things in their true perspective. We are shown very lovingly but definitely when we are "off the beam" and being uncaring and difficult in our relationships. At first when we ask for guidance from the Higher Self it is hard to be still. The more we practice the easier it becomes. Meditation is not just soaking in that inner peace. It is quieting the mind, feelings and body so we can touch that Real Self and learn to listen to the intuitions and impressions that come. Sometimes they come in meditation; sometimes the guidance comes floating in when we are busy in the world of appearance. But come it will if we ask. We have to ask if we would receive. This is because we were given free will and no higher force will intrude on us. The door has to be opened from within.

A meditation exercise that stemmed from an inner mystery school was shared with me, and I share it with others. It is an exercise in consciousness, so it uses our creative imagination – "image in." If we could have any place on the planet as our special sanctuary – our secret garden – where would we go when the world was too much with us? Where would we go to meet our Higher Self? Some have picked a chapel, others are placed in the woods, others go to the sea, others to the mountains. Once the decision is made, keep the sanctuary always in the same place. At first it is difficult to hold it in your consciousness, but stay with it. It took me about a year before it became a reality within me. In thought I built a chapel on a high hill overlooking the sea. The skies are always blue and it is always summer there. I stole the golden cross from the altar in Trinity Church in Boston. I took the Rose Window from the Notre Dame in Paris. No one ever missed them, for I took the psychic replicas of them. Each

15

morning when I went into meditation I would go to that holy place. There I would envision meeting my High Self and asking for guidance for the day. I always took my "Subby" with me and we would kneel before that inner alter and feel the healing power of the High Self flowing through us. I was given this exercise when I was too young a disciple to realize is potency or its power. I know now that the next dimension is a thought-built world, and at the chapel and place is a reality in that inner world. It helped me to concentrate and gave my mind something to do. That is the purpose of the mantras which are given to Eastern students. Mantras and visualizations, held in the third eye center (above the root of the nose in the forehead), quiet and steady the mind. After I used this method for a year, whenever things became hectic or agitated in the outer world I could shut my eyes and in a second of time be in that inner sanctuary. I could pick up that power and peace, and come back to the world fortified and regenerated. No one ever knew I had left. There is no time on the inner dimensions, not as we know it here.

Let me share with you some teaching on guidance which I received from my teacher in the early days of my discipleship:

DIVINE GUIDANCE

I wish I could sufficiently impress on you the necessity for utter an unquestioning obedience to the Voice Within. The master who seeks to use a human vehicle must be able to depend upon it. It must not fail him. Your master cannot always stop to explain his plan to you. In the first place, to do so would be to expose it to the opposition of those forces which ignorantly opposed the Light. Then again, his plan would often be utterly incomprehensible to the human personality, who at most sees but a few of the countless threads that are being used to weave a wondrous garment. It matters not that the direction which the Master gives you is not comprehensible to you; your path lies in trusting obedience. Many who are great in the eyes of the world are used by the Masters whenever they will respond, but too often they are too much concerned about some excellent scheme of their own to heed the Master's voice when its purpose is not understood. Such people may do much for man and for themselves, but they cannot be depended upon to do the Master's work.

The obedience must be instant an unequivocal. At first it is hard to listen and catch the Master's voice; but the facility grows with practice. One must seek guidance, not once or twice a day, but constantly. It doth not avail to ask God to keep you from mistakes unless you listen constantly for His Voice. At first you wander oft, and have to return repeatedly, and seek guidance anew. But through constant, quiet vigilance there comes a time when you walk with the Master as a constant presence.

It is not assumed that you will always infallibly interpret the Master's voice. Much of the human enters into distort, especially in the early stages of your training. Yet you may be sure that if you have erred in any vital matter, in bringing through your direction, the Master will quickly correct it.

The tests of obedience and responsiveness are very subtle. You must be proven unfailingly reliable if the Master is to depend on you for any very vital work. Many are willing, many are able, many are faithful, but so few are dependable. You would be astounded could you see upon how slight a thread the greatest decisions often hang.

When you ask for guidance, reach up to the very highest Being, however you may wish to term Him; and let Him guide you through whatever Master he may wish. Listen closely, for the answer is always dim at first, because your mind so quickly intrudes. Then reason not for or against the directions, but obey. One is often confused between two impressions. In such a case, it is usually wise is to write your request for guidance; in fact, it is always wise to ask for your guidance in writing until such time as the awareness of the Master's presence has grown into an abiding consciousness. Writing occupies the intellect, focuses the attention, and clears the mind for the direction to be more definitively received. Write whatever comes, even if it be but a word at a time. Constant listening clears the channel. There is no other way. The student must learn to trust his own inner voice. Often, false humility leads one virtually to say, "Nothing can come through me. I know you made me, God, but you can't do anything with me." This attitude is not only a self-betrayal, but a betrayal of the Father Himself, who seeks to manifest through you and through all of his children. Do not fight against this Inner Voice, but trust and listen until clear grows the Voice and plain the Path.

Sometimes you can look back and see the significance of a direction you have followed. But often you cannot see, and only know that by your obedience you have been serving, even tho' you know not how. You will very soon find proof abundant that your guidance thus sought is unfailing and divine. But the proof comes when you seek it not. You cannot ask for it. Utter faith is the first requisite of discipleship.

It may seem at first a trying path to follow; but it soon reveals itself as the only sure and happy way, and really the easiest of all. Auto release of the self-will, and listening obedience, brings a tranquility and a freedom from struggle and doubt, that cannot be measured. And no self-choice could bear a fraction of the interest of a life so dedicated. One daily watches a drama unfold in which one is both actor and spectator. And the rhythm of one's life becomes secure."

Being a very impulsive creature, it was difficult for me at first to know the difference between what was coming to me as guidance and what was pure impulse. For quite some time I didn't know for sure. When I asked my teacher how I would know which was which, she said, "For a while you won't know. Once you have dedicated yourself and agreed to go God's way, follow every impulse or intuition that comes to you. If eight out of ten times it's impulse, so what? The other two times may be guidance and you will not want to miss the guidance for it may be important." It wasn't very long before it was proven to me. I had a friend, Helen, who lived near me, who was very sick, and no doctor seemed to know what was wrong with her. I had another friend named Louise who lived in the western part of the state. She was a psychic and very accurate in her predictions. I was writing her a letter one afternoon and just as I finished the letter, I had an impression to add a P.S. to it: "Louise, Helen is quite sick and very depressed. She has great faith in what you say so would you drop her a note and cheer her up? It would mean a great deal to her."

About ten days afterward Helen went to the hospital and the condition was cleared up, and once again Helen was her cheery self. When I went to the hospital to see her, Helen said, "I received a letter from Louise that saved my life."

"What do you mean?"

"One afternoon I had reached the point where I couldn't go on any more. I had been saving my sleeping pills and decided I was going to use them all. I was so tired of pain and depression. I had just come into the hall and was going to go up the stairs when the mailman came up on the porch and put a letter in the slot. It fell on the floor at my feet. It was a letter from Louise telling me not to be discouraged, that within three days I'd be in the hospital and the condition would be cleared up. I sat on the stairs and cried and cried. If that letter hadn't come at that moment it would have been too late."

Inside I said, "Thank you, God." What I thought was an impulse was really guidance. From that time on I followed my impressions, and as time went on more and more of them proved to be guidance.

At first, going God's way is walking in what we call blind faith. If we keep going on in trust, we soon have proof that if we follow our inner impressions, they will always work out right. The learning to listen and obey opens the door to such a glorious and beautiful life.

Many people have said, "Well I pray. But what is the difference between prayer and meditation?" Meditation is listening to the Godself; prayer is talking to Him, and too often it is asking for something but not taking time to listen for the response. Do you call a beloved friend on the telephone, talk to him and then hang up before you've listened to what he has to say?

Through the years the prayer I have used and taught to others is, "Give me conscious contact with my Higher Self that I may more wisely obey and the better serve." With most of us it is not total surrender even if we think it is. In my own case each surrender proved to be only partial. Yet another had to be made. At last I reached the point where there was nothing else to rely on except the Inner Self.

Someone wrote a poem about this very thing, a definite and authentic experience in which she found herself hanging at the end of a rope. She was clutching it with all her strength in order to save herself from dropping into a bottomless abyss. She seemed to hear a voice saying, "Let go of the rope!" But she was afraid to do so for apparently it would mean her destruction. This is what we all have to face at some time or other – the death of ourselves, or all we cherish – or so it seems. At last, however, she let go, and immediately felt herself caught in the arms of God. She had solved the mystery. She knew the inner meaning of the words, "Let go and let God." By being willing to lose her life (to give it up) she had found it. Not by resistance, but by acceptance to we find the way Home. Willingness, not willfulness, is the way.

CHAPTER IV

OUR FATHER WHO ART IN HEAVEN

This prayer is one of the most powerful prayers in the world today. I have seen the conscious use of this prayer release earthbound souls, heal and restore an obsessed boy to radiant mental health, and act as a protective force in so many ways. Use it when you are in danger or sense evil around you, or when you are afraid. You can prove its power for yourself. Let us take it apart, sentence by sentence and examine its meaning. After meditating on its meaning in this manner for more than a year, it is painful to hear anyone recite its word words parrot-like, without any thought as to the real meaning of the prayer.

OUR FATHER WHO ART IN HEAVEN

"Ours," not yours, not mine, but" ours," i.e. everyone's collectively, together. "Father" is the positive pole of our own spirit, a positive outgoing energy that is in every one of us. It is the Lord or High Self in each and every one of us. That is the part of us that knows the unity of all Life. That Self was meant to be the outgoing expression of our real Self. We reversed our poles, making the personality (the unlit self) the positive pole and forced the real Self to take a back seat. The High Self was meant to be the expressor, and the personality the receiver, of the guidance that could be ours for the asking.

When Jesus said, "I am my Father are One; if ye have known me you have known the Father," he was telling us that his personality had become the servant of the Father (his High Self, or Lord) and that it was that Self that was using his personality as a channel. Jesus had given up his personal will to let the Father's will be done through him. When he reached that stage of surrender, he became Jesus, the Christ. The word "Christ" (or Krishna in Hindu terms) means "anointed one." Remember the picture, "The Light of the World," in which Christ stands at the door, knocking? The artist who painted it must have been an illumined soul. How many have been aware that there is no knob on the outside of the door? It can only be opened from within. When we use the Lord's Prayer, we are invoking the power of our own High Self which resides within us. Words alone, without feeling, will not bring us into contact with the Essential Being within us. When we men what we say, things always happen.

HALLOWED BE THY NAME

Our names are our nature, as per our signature or vibration. Before we come into a physical body, we have picked the name we will be called by on earth. It is a different name in each lifetime and carries a vibratory keynote. Our true spiritual name is not known to us on earth until we are able to make contact with the Creator in full consciousness. Then we are given our spiritual signature. The name "Jesus Christ" is one of the most powerful names, not only on earth but on the inner side of life. Through actual experience I have found that it truly is the name before whom all must bow. The next time you are going through a crisis, try repeating that name over and over again within yourself. The forces which are not of light cannot stand the vibration of that name and have to flee.

THEY KINGDOM COME. THY WILL BE DONE ON EARTH AS IT IS IN HEAVEN.

Heaven is within us. It always has been there. It never left us. It may be unclaimed, but it awaits recognition. Earth represents the personality whenever it is mentioned in the scriptures. Heaven represents our Real Self, the eternal and forever part of divinity. When that Will is allowed to take over the personal self, then truly "I and my Father are one," and we can say with Jesus, "If ye know me ye have known the Father." If we did not have love, peace, harmony and light at the center of our Being, we never we could never manifest it. It is always there waiting to be invited into the life we live on earth.

In this part of the prayer we are asking for heaven to become fully in manifest on earth (in the personality) as it is already manifest in our High Self. Do not expect to have Heaven outside until you find it inside first. You are in Heaven when you are truly loving. That is what Heaven really is: Love.

The young people have a saying I love: "You are beautiful!" They are not talking of outward beauty. If there was not a beautiful being within each and every one of us how could we recognize it in anyone else? Whenever the scriptures speak of "earth," substitute the word "personality" (the earth part of us), and you will know its true meaning. "The heavens (the High Self) declare the glory of God; The earth (the personality) showeth forth his handiwork." The Lord is in His holy temple; let all the earth (the personality) keep silent before Him. When the Will of the Father (the Real Self) is done here in the "earth-part" of us we have accomplished the lessons we needed to learn in this earth school and can truthfully say: "Not I, but the Father, doeth the Work."

GIVE US THIS DAY OUR DAILY BREAD.

We are asking for Manna, the vital force of life, to sustain us, to nourish the mind, the feelings and the body. Not for tomorrow, or for the day after tomorrow, but for this day. Most of the anxieties man deals with in the world today are caused by worrying about tomorrow and what we might need. Where is tomorrow? Have we ever caught up with it? Bread for today is what we ask. The next day's supply will be there if we ask, believing, when that day comes. When I have felt a sense of lack, I have used a sentence called to call day mantram to remind me of something I was forgetting: "My heavenly Father owns the Universe and every need will be supplied." It always has been so. Miracles *do* follow miracles and I have seen them manifested, not only in my own life, but in the lives of so many others. Jesus said: "Prove me. I will open the windows of Heaven and pour forth to you such a blessing your hands will not be able to contain it." It will prove to be more beautiful and wonderful than anything we could ever expect. This is especially so when it is something to be shared with others. The subconscious learns by repetition and if any mantram is said over and over again within one's self, it works. We create our own conditions. If we have faith in good, good happens. If we have faith in negative things, negative things have to happen.

FORGIVE US OUR DEBTS AS WE FORGIVE OUR DEBTORS.

Do we? Are there any of us who do not need to be forgiven? Do we want to be forgiven? Do we want our debts cleared? Can we be forgiving, for giving *up* our resentment, and the bitterness, that is eating us up inside? Can we offer it up on the inner altar of our being? A person hurts us. Time passes. The person changes, for the law of the world of appearance is change. If we are unloving in our consciousness, we continue to hold that person to the old concepts and patterns. We thereby bind ourselves to a situation that harms us far more than it does the other person. We refuse to allow the wound to heal. We keep picking at the sore in our consciousness so that it does not heal. Infection sets in. Who is sick.? The other fellow? No, we are.

How can we get rid of the infection? Through the realization that everyone, bar no one, does the only thing he or she can do with a consciousness he has at any particular moment in time and space. When he knows better, he will do better. This "knowing" is not of the mind. NEVER MIND. We say it all the time and never hear what it says. "Real" understanding is realization and comes from the heart, not the mind. Look back in your own life. Isn't there much you would change where your actions were concerned if you had been more understanding? This is true for all of us. Do not bind another person to his worst moments if you do not want to bind yourself to your worst ones. Forgive yourself as you forgive others.

My mind goes back to a spring evening in my studio in Boston. I was conducting a class for my spiritual family. We were through with our discussion and ready to have our meditation, when I heard myself saying, "When it comes to the Lord's prayer, if there is anyone here who cannot forgive, he should omit this line: "Forgive us our debts as we forgive our debtors." Do not be a hypocrite. The honest. Your High Self will honor you for it." After the meditation was over and the people had left, a friend stayed behind with a newcomer she had brought with her that night. This is what the newcomer said: "You were talking to me tonight. For twenty years I have hated my father because his cruelty was instrumental in causing my mother's death. I said I would never forgive him, and I would never pray again. I haven't lived a good life in the past twenty years. Tonight in the meditation I was healed and able to forgive my father." Her voice broke and she started to cry. "When I forgave him inside myself I heard my beloved mother's voice say, "Now darling, God has forgiven you."

Then something happened that had never happened before nor since. The room was filled with the most heavenly scent of roses. Never have I smelled such a fragrance, although there were no roses in the room.

LEAVE US NOT INTO TEMPTATION BUT DELIVER US FROM EVIL.

After meditating on this prayer for a year it was given to me to understand that the forces of Light never *lead* us into temptation. *It was a wrong translation.* The forces of Light do step aside when it is necessary for us to be tested but they never test us nor lead us into evil. Love never tests. There are times when the forces of Light allow the negative forces to test us in order for us to know our own strengths and our own weaknesses. What is "evil"? Reverse the word and you have "live." Evil is living in reverse. All energy is pure. It is how we use it that labels it. A fire in a fireplace can be a blessing. The same fire in the wrong place and out of control can burn a house down. Is fire evil then? Any virtue carried to excess becomes a vice, just as every vice has a virtue hidden in it. The High Self can deliver us from evil *if* we ask for that help. Whether it is "love" or "evil" ultimately depends on how we use the energy.

FOR THINE IS THE KINGDOM AND THE POWER AND THE GLORY

Oh, how I love that sentence! It takes us off the hook. We can flow freely through life knowing where the power lies. It takes away egotism for we know that of ourselves we can do nothing. It puts the power and the glory where they belong — in the "Kingdom of Heaven

28

Consciousness." We are but channels, instruments that can be used by the power if we do not try to appropriate it for ourselves. I often wondered why the Catholic Church left this sentence out of their liturgy. Now I know. This is pure Qubalah, the esoteric part of the Judaic tradition. It is tied with the three sephiroth on the Tree of Life: Hod (the power, Mercury), Netzach (the glory, Venus) and Malkuth (the kingdom of earth). The time will come when it will truly be "on earth as it is in heaven."

FOREVER AND EVER.

This means the internal, never-ending pattern and design — so let it be. Amen.

CHAPTER V

THOUGH CHRIST A THOUSAND TIMES

If the teachings of Jesus in the scriptures cannot be applied to our livingness in the Here and Now, of what use are they? In my spiritual ongoing I wanted to know what the parables and teachings really meant, and how they could be applied to everyday life. Knowing that energy follows thought, and that if we asked inwardly, we would receive, I meditated on the parables until the answers came

One story that puzzled me was the conversation Jesus had with the woman of Samaria who was drawing water from a well. You will find it in the fourth chapter of the Gospel of Saint John. Jesus told the woman she had five husbands and that the man she now she had now was not her husband. Then he offered her the "living waters." This story hung around the outskirts of my consciousness and would not go away. I quieted my outside self, and went to the High Self to ask what it meant. The answer came. The five husbands were the five senses, and the man she had now was the sixth sense. This was the psychic sense and was no more reliable than the other senses. The living waters that the Lord of her being could give her were the seventh sense, the intuitive knowledge that would come from the Inner Being, the "forever" part of us.

Because the veils are now getting thinner between the earth plane and the psychic levels, many are becoming conscious of their psychic sense. It can be cultivated if one so wishes, but it is not always reliable, and can lead one down the primrose path of illusion on the psychic or astral planes if one is not cautious. "Seek ye *first* the Kingdom of Heaven and all else shall be added unto you." From the higher spiritual levels comes the living water. This is the intuitive sense which is dependable and will not let us down. If we seek the highest and purest help when we need information on the inner levels, we will be protected.

The ouija board and automatic writing are extremely dangerous for some people because they can lead to obsession and mental instability. There was one whom I warned about developing his psychic sense. Unfortunately, he would not listen. After a stay in a mental institution he realized the advice was sound. There are a few who have been chosen to work in the psychic field. They have been protected by higher forces. Others are not.

Another parable that intrigued me was the one about the disciples out in the boat during a storm. (Matthew, Chapter 8). The disciples were in deep trouble. Jesus was fast asleep in the hold. Why? Didn't their Lord know their boat was being battered by the wind and the storm and they were in danger of sinking? Fine Master, he was! Sound asleep when they needed Him. What is this story trying to tell us? Not until we awaken the Christ in our own hearts will the storms of life subside. Only that Self that dwells in every man has the power to say to our stormy emotions: "Peace, be still. Be wrapped in perfect peace." Another important truth is hidden here. The High Self must be invited in and asked for help. As long as we think we can handle everything for ourselves we are on our own.

At first, I was bothered by the parable of the talents in the 25th Chapter of Matthew. Why should one man be given five talents, and having brought back five more, be blessed? Meanwhile, the one who was given only one talent, and hugged it to himself so that he would not lose it, had his one talent taken away from him? It did not seem fair. After much pondering I realized the true meaning of it all. What we don't use, we lose. This is true on all levels of existence. Even in our physical bodies this holds true. If we stay in bed for two weeks without using our legs, what happens when we try to walk? We are unable to. If we refuse to be loving and to share love, our capacity for love atrophies. Every one of us is born with a talent of some kind. If it lies dormant and is not used, what good is it?

In my work as a counselor I have seen so many people with talents they are not using. These talents represent buried treasures that are unrecognized within the individual. One day a man came to see me. He came under protest to please his wife. He was in a very depressed state. His wife thought I could help him. He did not think so. The first thing he said to me was: "You can't do anything for me, but I promised Alice I would come and here I am." I smiled and said, "Maybe I can't, but perhaps God can." He did not know that my silent partner (my High Self) and his High Self could get together and give us the answer. He was sixty-nine years old, retired and living on Social Security benefits. His income was not sufficient to meet their needs, so his wife had to work. This bothered him for he was a proud man. His feeling that he was a failure and that life was over for him was making him very depressed.

When I had taken down his birthdate and set up his blueprint (his horoscope) I saw there a buried treasure, a talent, hidden deep within him which had never been used. He did not know what was there. He had been a sea captain up in the Puget Sound area and in Alaskan waters. He had had many experiences in the northwest dealing with the Eskimos and the Indian tribes. He had a tremendous gift for telling stories as well as for writing.

If he would only use his talent, not only would he get out of the doldrums, but he would be financially secure. I knew that if he went home and put his adventures on paper, his whole life would change. I did not know at that time he used to captivate all the neighborhood children by telling them stories of his adventures.

My silent partner and I never worked harder to get an idea across than that day. I told him that if he did what I told him I wanted the second copy of his first book when it came off the press. Alice could have the first one. And he and Alice could take me to dinner the night they brought it to me. He was in a much better mood after our talk and he grinned. I told him his first book would make him financially independent, but he would go on to write two more books after that that one. Can you imagine how my heart saying the night Alice and he came to bring me a copy of his book and to take me out to dinner? That week in the Boston Globe there was a story that carried the headline: MAN WRITES HIS FIRST NOVEL AT SEVENTY. He was able to go back to his beloved Puget Sound area to write two more books and end his days in the wilderness he loved. We all have unused talents. It has been stated that we only use five percent of our potential. Christopher Frye had a line in his "Sleep of Prisoners" I have never forgotten: "Oh God. The marvelous wings unfurled, buried in the heart."

I have thought much about the birth of the Christchild, Jesus. It is symbolic of the birth of the Christ Consciousness within us. When the angel came to Mary and told her she was going to conceive the Christ, what was her response? "Behold the handmaiden of the Lord. Be it done unto me according to His will." How many times have I said that within myself when I have felt my self-will rising. More times than I could count. This is the first step on the journey Home for the spiritual a spirant; giving up the self-will and letting God's will be done. It is a long time from conception to birth. That seed has to have its growth in the darkness before it can come to birth in the light. Before a baby can be born, the waters that have enclosed it in the darkness have to break. Water has always been the symbol of our emotions. Before the

Christ child can come to birth in the Manger of our hearts, we have to break free from our emotions.

The waters break. The child is born. Where? There is no room in the inn; no room in the world of glamour, noise and confusion. He is born in a stable, among the animals. All the animals in that stable were domesticated. The animals in us have to be domesticated before that Christ principle can come to birth in us. Who else was in that stable? Only the very humble, the shepherds, and the very wise, the Magi. This story is as true today as it was two thousand years ago.

"Though Christ a thousand times in Bethlehem be born
And is not born in you, His birth has been in vain."

CHAPTER VI

PRAYER AND MEDITATION

If we better understand the universal principles, we could make better use of the cosmic laws that govern the operation of this planet. Man's cooperation with those laws is a vital necessity for God operates in the world of appearance *through* man. It is the God Power (or whatever you want to call that creative energy) that supplies the energy. The energy has to have a human instrument through which it can manifest. We are free agents. We may cooperate or not as we choose. The God Power does not operate on earth except through the great elements of nature. Nature brings forth its increase of one kind or another, but God does not save a person from drowning or from a fire if there is no other human being at hand through which He can operate.

Prayer is talking to God. Meditation is quieting the outside self and listening to what God has to say. We do not call a friend on the telephone and hang up before we get an answer. We do not always receive the answer in the quiet time but that prepares the way for us to receive the answer. Many times, I would receive Light while I was busy doing some mundane task in my daily life on a problem I had taken to my Higher Self and left at that inner altar. If every thought is registered on the ether, as it is, then every prayer goes forth too. It is not always answered on the outer levels, but no sincere prayer is prayed in vain. For a long time, I pondered about the reason some prayers were answered and some were not. It was only after I found out that the subconscious self was the intermediary between the High Self and the conscious self that I understood. If the little self felt guilty or ashamed it would not carry the prayer to the High Self. Jesus said, "You pray and you pray amiss." I pondered over that statement for a long time. When we pray we should visualize the prayer as answered, see the healing as done, and give thanks that it is accomplished. When we see the negatives in any situation, we increase their power for, as mentioned previously, energy follows thought. The High Self sees the result of the answered prayer and sometimes, in mercy, it does not give us the answer that we think we want. We do not have the wisdom, especially in our early years, to know what is for our highest good.

In my younger years, like many others, I loved someone that I thought would be the most wonderful companion I could have. If the prayer had been answered as I wanted, I would have been a very miserable and unhappy person. In my counseling this problem comes up again and again. An individual is in love with someone and wants the experience to be successful and permanent.

The astrological horoscopes tell a story of how the energies will work between the two people. Sometimes the blueprints show clearly it would be the worst thing that could happen if they join forces. Sometimes the individuals listen, and time shows the wisdom of their decision. Sometimes the individuals find out through experience and come back to tell me they wish they had listened. My reply has been: "If this experience was important for your soul growth nothing anyone could say would have made any difference. You needed the experience and so you made the right choice no matter how difficult it has been. Now do not run out on it. Lift it through prayer into Light and Love. Then you will never need such a painful experience again. Turn it over to your High Self and let God's Will be done in this situation. The experience always works out rightly for both parties, if that is done.

Perhaps personal experience of prayer power can help. Our first meditation and prayer group started a long time ago. We were neophytes of the most ignorant kind but we wanted to go God's way and decided to experiment and see for ourselves whether prayer and meditation were indeed effective. We met once a week and had a rap session followed by a meditation. (Incidentally, that format is still used today by our group.) Always as part of our meditation time we prayed for the healing for others. The answers to the prayers were amazing. Group energy proved to be more powerful than we had ever dreamed it would be.

We had been meeting a short while when a telephone call came from Julyan, a member of the group. "Isabel, I know we don't meet until Wednesday and this is only Monday but there is a friend of mine who is scheduled in the hospital to have her leg amputated in the morning. She has a very high fever, and the doctor said that only amputation would save her life. Do you suppose a few of us could get together at my house tonight and pray for her?" "Of course." Seven people gathered at Julyan's home that evening. Two of the participants were new to our group and had never prayed. Only Julyan knew the person who we were putting into God's hands for healing. We were so new at this business we were not sure what to do. We decided to get quiet, hold hands in a circle and ask God to use us as channels. We asked him to pour his healing power through us to the girl in the hospital. We thanked God for the healing as we finished. It was nine o'clock when we sat down and we were in prayer for ten minutes. Then we had coffee, conversation and went home. The next afternoon Julyan called me on the telephone. His voice was so excited. "Isabel, at nine o'clock last night my friend's temperature went down to normal, her leg was healed, and they are sending her home today." It was our first experience in praying for someone that most of us did not know. It was such a joy to know that as inexperienced as we were, and as little as we knew, God could use us. Many miracles have happened since then in our healing group that have proven to us that prayer works.

It is the unselfish prayers that seemed to be the most successful. When we deal with prayer power, we realize we do not have to pray for ourselves. We become channels for that Power and as it flows through us our needs are automatically answered. The flow of energy and healing clears the channel as it flows through. At first, when I was a spiritual student I would sit down and at the beginning of my quiet time with my High Self I would plunge into praying for others. But I learned. After a while I learned to get quiet first, making the contact with the High Self before I could bring those for whom I felt responsible to the inner altar in my heart. Once I had brought them to that altar it was ALL right. I kept a prayer book and in it the names of those for whom I was praying. As the prayers were answered I crossed off their names and added others. In a year's time that little book bore witness to many such miracles. It amazed me. Without that little book I would not have realized the power of God to work out so many difficulties. Not one of those prayers were for myself but things in my own life became better and better. All my days were beginning to be 'pleasant ones at all my paths were peace.'

Daily meditations are of great importance. If we start the day with a quiet time, asking for contact with that Eternal Self within us, and for guidance for that day it will be so. The day will be far more productive. That is learning to dwell in the secret place of the most High. Read the 91st psalm. The promise is there. Never in the history of the planet has it been so important to find our inner center and function from that center. In the last five years meditation and healing groups have sprung up all over the planet. Some of the groups and teachers are making money for their endeavors, but there are others who know God is not a materialist. There are many little groups everywhere, unhonored and unsung, who are getting together to send forth healing vibrations and are serving as channels of Love and Light. It is not the organized religions that are holding the forces of darkness at bay. It is the young people and those young of heart that are bringing in the light and the true age of brotherhood. In spite of the doomsday prophets and the gloomy predictions of those who are the ignorant tools of the dark brothers we are coming into the greatest period this planet has ever known.

At the present time (1976) we are in the wrecking time where all the old corruption and the hidden evil that has been undercover for so long is coming to the surface to be cleansed and redeemed. Evil in high places is being exposed as never before and the end is not in sight. If we judge by appearances the picture seems dismaying. But the poisons must come to the surface before they can be illuminated. Collectively and personally it is testing time. That which is no longer valuable and usable is on its way out. After the wreckers come the builders. They are on their way. Every little group that comes together once a week to meditate and pray together will be used by the forces of Light to bring in the new energy that can redeem the planet. Leaner or lifter, healer or herder, the choice is yours.

CHAPTER VII

EXPLAINING GOD AND LIFE TO CHILDREN

Upon a time in the long long ago, before this planet which we call Earth was born, we all lived in a beautiful place very far away. Some call it Heaven and some called it the Garden of Eden. It was very beautiful. It still exists, and it is still beautiful. In that place everyone loved everyone else and there were no hurts or troubles of any kind. There never are when people are truly loving. We were shining Spirits and God was the shiniest Spirit of all. Our Spirit is still part of us and is our Guardian Angel who watches over us from the time we come down to earth until we go back to our Heavenly Home. Let's call that angel in us the Big Me. That Big Me is always there inside us, even if we can't see it with our earth eyes. We can feel it when we are very quiet and good, and very loving. When we ask it to help us it will. That is, if we are loving. Being kind and loving opens the inside door so that the Spirit, our Guardian Angel, can come in and give us the help we need.

Let's call the Me that everyone sees the Outside Me. That's the everyday self that gets up in the morning, plays, or goes to school, and lives in the outside world. Then there is the little self that lives inside, called the "Little Me." That Little Me doesn't think but it feels everything. The Outside Me has to do the thinking for the Little Me that lives inside because it isn't very big and it has a lot to learn. The Outside Me has to be its teacher. When that Little Me wants to be mean, on loving or angry, we have to talk to it and say, "You mustn't misbehave. If you want us to be happy you have to be good." Every day we must tell our Little Me how much we love it and how much God loves it too. Sometimes it is naughty because it doesn't feel loved or it's afraid. We must tell it about the Big Me that loves us both. That Little Me can grow up to be a beautiful me if we help it by training it to be loving to everyone.

It's the Big Me that helps us to understand what God is. The Big Me is the part of us that knows what God is for it is part of him. God is the Spirit that is everywhere there is life. He is in the air we breathe, the water we drink, in the trees, the flowers, the mountains, the hills and the earth on which we live. He is in us too. He is life, and life is energy. Wherever there is energy God's Spirit is working. You can't find Him with your mind. You have to feel Him in your heart. Imagine a tremendous ball of fire of energy going round and round in space. It goes so fast it throws off sparks of itself. It is like the sparklers on the 4th of July. One of those sparks or little lights landed inside each one of us. So we are part of that energy we call God or Spirit. That is the same energy that is in the great big energy, but we are tiny bits of it. At the very center of every one of us is that Light and Love. That is the God part of us.

We wanted to make that light in us brighter and brighter and to know more about what God is. In order to learn anything, we have to go to school. The planet we live on is a school. That Light within us had to have a body to wrap around it so we could come down to the earth school. Up there in Heaven where there is only Love and Light, we know we are part of everyone else and everything else. Up there we know we are part of God and each other. It is when we come down here and get into bodies that we forget who we really are. We may think we are different and better or worse than anyone else but we aren't.

Why did we want to come down here when everything was so beautiful up there? We wanted to have free will and use it so someday we could be like God and know how to create universes and stars and planets and know how to run them as well as how to make them. We wanted to do what God did. First we had to learn how to create. We would make many mistakes before we learn to be like God. It would take us a long time and a great deal of education before we would learn to create beautiful things. We had to practice for we couldn't be allowed to mess up Heaven with things that weren't beautiful. So the great Spirit we call God gave us a planet which is like a huge spaceship floating in space. We call it the earth. On this spaceship we are all given the opportunity to learn how to live and how to love. Some of us learn more quickly than others because some of us want so much to know. Some of us are lazy and do not want to learn. It is like our classes in school. Some people study harder and learn quicker and go to the head of the class. Others fool around and don't pay attention to what the teacher is trying to tell them so they learn at a slower pace.

Many lifetimes ago when we first started, we had a good body. God told us to take care of it for it was our temple in which we would live while we were on earth. We were given free will, so it was up to us whether we would take care of it or not. We could keep it clean or we could let it get dirty and messy. We could give it good food so it would be healthy. If we gave it the wrong food, it would get sick. We would be the ones who had to live in it, so it was up to us. If we took care of our bodies, we would earn a good body the next time we came to earth. If we didn't take care of it we might have to live in a sick body or a crippled one. God didn't do it to us: we did to ourselves. Our bodies are like a house that we live in while we are on earth. Every night when we go to sleep, we leave the body so it can get a rest from us and build up its energy again. We go back to Heaven an if, as we go to sleep, we tell ourselves to remember where we went and what we did, we may wake up in the morning knowing all about it. Some children have playmates from Heaven who come and play with them, so they won't be lonely. Grownups can't see them, so they say they aren't there. But children know and see them. Some children see colors around people, and they think everyone sees them, but everyone doesn't see them. The colors tell whether people are sad or happy or angry or loving. Colors tell what the person is like inside.

This planet is like a school. We start in the first grade and after we learn all the lessons we need to learn in the first grade, we have a vacation. When we go back to school after vacation, we go to the second grade and have other lessons to learn. And so we go through each grade with more and harder lessons to learn on the way. And we always have a vacation between each grade before we go on to the next grade. That's what death is, leaving the body and going back to Heaven on a vacation to have a rest and a change. After a rest in our real Home we come back to school again. Before coming back to earth, the everyday Me that is coming down to earth talks it over with the great Spirit and the Big Me and decides who it is going to pick for a father and mother and what it is going to learn in the grade it is going to be in. Each grade is a lifetime, and it takes many lifetimes and many experiences before we are ready to graduate from school. When we do graduate, we don't have to come back to earth school again. We can go to other places that are so much nicer and happier, for there is more love there.

Down here on earth we are learning how to love. We haven't learned very much about love yet. If we had, there would be no more wars on earth or troubles in families. Perhaps we have come down here to help the planet by being more loving ourselves. It is the people who aren't loving who need love the most. We don't have to *like* them. Liking has to be earned. But love is different, because love is God using us (if we want Him to!) to help bring more Love to earth. Because God gave us free will when we came to earth, we have to invite Him to use us as channels of Love. If we are selfish or hateful, He can't use us because our channels are choked up and Love can't get through. Every morning when we wake up, if we'd say this little prayer, we could be helpers not hurters:

> "Great Spirit, thank you for this day. May my Big Me show me what it wants me to do today. Help me to be kind and loving and helpful to everyone I see today. Help me to teach my Little Me how to be loving too. Help the Little Me, deep down inside of me, to know how much I love it and help us both to know the Big Me is our guardian angel and loves us too."

You can give your Little Me a name if you like. Ask inside what it would like to be called.

Our bodies are new each time we come to earth, but the person who lives in the body isn't new. Some of us have had more lifetimes (grades) on earth than others. This is the reason some children know more than others. Sometimes children can teach their parents for some have lived more lifetimes and are older inside than people whose bodies are much older. Sometimes the Big Me in children is very close to them and tells them things inside that are really true. That's because they learned about the Big Me in other lifetimes. They learn to ask it for help, and they learn to love that Big Me very much.

When God, the Great Spirit, gave us free will before any of us came to earth, He told us we could do as we wished, but that we would have to be responsible for what we did. He said everything, good or bad, that we did would come back to us. If we did a good deed, or thought a good thought, it would go out, make a circle and come back to us. If we hurt anyone, then that hurt has to come back to us too. People who understand this truth call it the law of Karma. If in one lifetime we have been a mean father or mother, then in the next lifetime we choose to be born to a mean father or mother, so that we will know what it is like and we will never be like that again. That is how we learn.

So many people blame God for what happens to them. God does not do things to them. They do it to themselves. The Outside Me doesn't remember what it did, but the Big Me knows. Sometimes when we ask the Big Me why we have troubles, if we really want to know, the Big Me helps us to understand. When we understand the law of Karma, we do not blame anyone for our troubles, not even ourselves. Whatever we have done we know we did the only thing we could do for we did not know any better. God forgives us. We have to learn to forgive others as well as to forgive ourselves. We have to pay our dues. There are two ways of paying, and we have a choice. One is service and the other is suffering.

Each lifetime the Outside Me is new and so is the brain. That's why the Outside Me doesn't remember. But the Big Me and the little Me knows. Sometimes when we go to sleep at night and leave the body to go back to Heaven we can ask if we could see what we have done in other lifetimes. Then, when we wake in the morning, we may remember if the Big Me thinks we should.

When people we love die, we may not be able to see them, for they have left the body they lived in on earth. God has given them a new body in which to live in Heaven. We do not lose them, for every night when we go to sleep, we go to Heaven and are with them. They help the Big Me to take care of us. We never lose those we love. Love is forever, just as God is. When we have a vacation from the earth school and go back to Heaven for a rest, everyone we have loved who is in Heaven will be there to meet us. We will be going Home — to our heavenly home — and it will be a beautiful homecoming. All those whom we have loved who went there before us will be there.

Life for life is for living and for loving, no matter whether we are living in a earth body or living in a body of Light which is our Spirit

48

body. That Spirit body looks like the Outside Me but is much more beautiful and filled with Light. We will know each other in our Heavenly Home if we know each other here. Our Spirit body is never sick and it is never old. It just could not be. That is why some people who have been sick a long time are so happy when they drop off the old and worn out body and are living in their shining body of Light, and I've gone back to Heaven where there is no pain or trouble of any kind. Can't you imagine how happy they are?

All we take with us when we go back to our real Home is all that we have given away in Love and Service to others. Let us go forward into each day unafraid, for our Guardian Angel — the Big Me — goes with us if we ask it to. The Little Me is the companion and friend who lives in our hearts and will do so many things to help us if we learn to love it. Think to it and it will think back to you. It is a real pal when you make it so.

CHAPTER VIII

AND A LITTLE CHILD

Michael and Nancy were playing on the porch. They were cousins and lived next door to one another. Nancy was six years old and Michael was seven years in his body but much older in his soul. His mother was sewing in her chair near the window and heard them arguing. She listened and heard Michael say,

"Nancy, there are, too, seven heavens!"

"No there aren't. There's one heaven. We had it in Sunday School."

His mother put her head out of the window and said,

"Why do you say that, Michael?"

"Because there are."

"How do you know?"

"Mummy, when God wants me to know something God makes me think it. There *are* seven heavens; up in the highest heaven we are alivest of all. And, as we come down through the different heavens we get deader and deader. Down here we are deadest of all."

Could there be any more graphic description of the seven planes of consciousness?

There was another time when Michael was eating his breakfast and pondering about something. His mother asked him what he was thinking.

"I was wondering why people are afraid to die, Mummy. They die every night. Don't they know that the only difference between sleeping and dying is that when they die they forget to come back to their bodies in the morning?"

"What do you mean, Michael?"

"Well, the body wants to get rid of the person in it, so the person leaves it and goes to Heaven to give his body a rest. I got out of my body the other night and looked at it lying on the bed and I thought, 'Wouldn't it be funny if I didn't come back into it? It would shrink and wouldn't be of any more use.' I see you and Daddy over there in Heaven many times while your bodies are asleep, but you are both walking around as though you aren't fully awake."

"How do you know how to get out of your body, Michael?"

"The first time I did it, a lovely lady with colors all around her came and took me across the water and showed me how to go to Heaven."

"Did you get wet?"

"No, it wasn't wet water. It looked like water and it was shimmery, but it wasn't wet. After that I knew how to do it myself. I don't always go to Heaven. Sometimes I travel around the earth and see different places. The other night I was riding on a train. I was sitting beside a lady and she didn't know I was there. I could see in her mind, and she was very unhappy. She thought no one loved her and she was very sad. I sat there and told her God loved her, and I asked God to put His love all around her. I think He did because the colors around her that were dark grey changed into a pink kind of color. Mummy, do you know when you have been in Heaven in your sleep?"

"No, I don't Michael."

"It's when you wake up with a very happy feeling in the morning."

Michael's mother had a sick friend. Thinking that Michael had a more direct contact with God than she had, she asked him to pray for her friend. His answer was a nonchalant, "Sure." The next night she asked him again. He looked at her as though he was disgusted.

"Mummy, I asked God to do it last night. He is taking care of it. When I ask him for help, I don't say, 'God, do it, do it, do it!' She is all right."

What a blessing that Michael chose a family that would have some understanding and know that he was not fantasizing but talking Reality.

Recently, a mother who thought the child to whom she had given birth was weird, went to her priest to find out if she had a child with a mental problem. Luckily, her priest, being clairvoyant, knew all about reincarnation and knew the inner laws. The mother was a young soul, completely steeped in dogma and creed, but without consciousness of life and its real meaning. Her little boy was four years old. One day, she was irritated and cranky with him. He looked at her very seriously and said,

"If you don't stop being so cranky, I'm going back to my other mother."

"You never had another mother," she said. "I am the only mother you ever had."

"Oh no, you are not. I had another mother, and she was much nicer than you. She was never cross. We lived in a jungle. Everything was wonderful until a white man came to our hut and sold my father a gun. He didn't know how to use it. He was trying to make it work, and there was a big bang that killed my mother. She went back to Heaven. I was so lonesome for her that after a little while I went back to Heaven too. So if you aren't nice to me, I'll go back to Heaven and find my other mother."

Another day she was lying down with a headache. Tommy came to the door and she told him to go away because she had a headache. He said:

"I'll take your headache away. I was a doctor once, and I know how."

She thought she would humor him, so she said, "What do you want to do?"

He said, "Lie on your tummy and put your hands behind your back and put them together."

She did it. He put his little hands upon hers, and to her amazement her headache was gone.

"My headache's gone!" she said.

He looked at her rather surprised that she doubted him, and said, "Didn't I tell you it would be?"

Another incident that happened involved a young child and his grandmother, whom he loved very much. He was lying in his bed one night on the 1st floor of his home, and his grandmother was in her bed upstairs. He saw his grandmother leave her body and called to his mother.

"Granny has gone away, Mama. I think she's gone to Heaven."

"Nonsense, she's asleep in her bed upstairs!" said his mother.

"Go up and see, Mama. She's gone away. I saw her go."

The mother went upstairs and found that her mother had left her body and was what the world calls 'dead.'

Recently, a grandmother, brought up in the Jewish tradition, said that she was very upset by her four-year-old grandson. She said he kept asking her questions about God and why we were here and what we were here on earth for. She was unable to tell him for she didn't know. She is no different from many people in other faiths. Being brought up in dogma, creed and orthodoxy does not give the answers. The era of mere acceptance of traditional concepts is over. The children of today want to *know why*. Many of them do know more than their parents because they are older souls. In the Piscean Age that is waning we had to take things on faith. In the Aquarian Age that is coming in, to faith must be added knowledge and understanding. The young people want to know. "Seek and ye shall find; knock and the door shall be opened." This is just as true today as it has been all through the ages. In every question is hidden the answer.

CHAPTER IX

THE MATING GAME

One of the greatest hungers felt by people on this plant is the hunger for love. So few people have that need for love satisfied. This hunger causes more pain than any other need. It is understandable when we know that on the personality level, we are not complete in ourselves. We are not self-sufficient no matter how much we declare it and think we are. Only when the union is made between the soul and the spirit is the search over. Then the seeking on the outer level is no longer necessary. "GOD TOOK A SHINING SPIRIT: HALVED IT AND SAID, GO FORTH AND MAY THYSELF WHOLE."

So it all began. We separated, and part of that self came down into the darkness of earth and a part of us stayed upstairs in the higher realm and kept its contact with the Creator.

It takes a very long time for the self in the dark to realize that what we are looking for out here lies deep within us. Only through relationships, many of them painful, do we learn what love is all about. But every bit of love, no matter how small, that we give out is bringing us closer to the great love we will be submerged in someday. Love of any kind, whether it be for another human, or love for an animal, or love for an ideal, plays its part in our ongoing growth and development. Even though we may love unwisely it is better to love than not. For a long time, we think we love and proclaim it. Then the loved one does something we do not like, or love someone more than us and our love departs. Let us face it. Real love does not change even when the loved one is no longer there. It is not what we say that counts, though to be told we are loved is very sweet. It is what we do that tells the real story.

For many lifetimes we search for the other half of ourselves on the outer side of life. Sometimes we think we have found it. Then we find it was wishful thinking on our part because of our need and our hunger. It takes so long to find out that what we are searching for outwardly lies within us.

There is so much talk on the physical level about soul mates. One day while meditating and thinking about this aspect of life, I heard a sweet voice deep within me say, "The secret is hidden in the triangle." I have pondered much on this sentence. Could it be that the two aspects of ourselves — positive (masculine) and receptive (feminine) — are united in the Spirit where there is no duality. From the union of two forces a third force is always created Even if the results do not materialize on the physical plane. The marriage union of the highest nature on the physical level is the dimmest foreshadowing of the ecstasy of the Divine Marriage between the soul and the spirit. In the illumined ones this marriage has taken place. So they need no counterpart in the outer world. In speaking of his master my teacher told me that his guru had the body of a man and the breasts of a woman. He had become complete within himself. The highest masters have made this attainment and do not marry. When the positive and negative poles within an entity are united there is no need of a counterpart in the world of appearance. Until we attain that union there is a hunger and a yearning for completion. For many lifetimes this completion is sought in the world of appearance where it can only be a partial union. There is no perfection on the personality side of our natures. If there was we would not have to be here. This is a "learning to love" process on the outer level.

We must face another fact. For a long time, some of us find living a long and lonely road. While we are caught in our own selves, how can

58

we know what love is? How can we feel another person's needs and pain if we are too busy thinking about our own? We can isolate ourselves through our own self-centeredness and selfishness. Too often we blame the other person, not realizing we are projecting on others our own lack of lovingness. So often in counseling I have had people say, "I am not going to love for every time I do I get hurt. I am not going to get involved again. I loved him but he did not love me." Which one was enriched? The one who gave or the one who took? Have you ever read those beautiful lines in Longfellow's prose poem, "Evangeline?" Gabriel was taken away from her just before their wedding day. Though others loved her (for she was beautiful, within and without) her heart had been given to Gabriel. Her friends begged her to forget him for chances were very great that she would never find him again. Then did Evangeline answer:

"I cannot. When the heart goes before like a lamp and illuminates the darkness, much is made clear it that else lies hidden in darkness."

And the priest, her friend, said,

"Daughter, Thy God speaketh within thee. Talk not of wasted affection. Affection never was wasted. If it enrich not the heart of another, its waters, returning back to their springs, like rain, shall fill them full of refreshment. That which the fountain sends forth returns again to the fountain. Patience, accomplish thy labor, accomplish thy work of affection. Sorrow and silence are strong, patient endurance is godlike, purified, strengthened, perfected, and made more worthy of heaven."

Love is never wasted. We may love the wrong person or love unwisely, and this can bring pain. Nevertheless, it is through loving we learn and grow in wisdom. If we could only realize that pain is the other side of pleasure. You cannot have one without the other. When we are willing to accept the pain that goes with loving we learn what love and pain are all about. It is better to love and to get hurt than to close ourselves off from loving because of fear. If we were not a threefold being it would be easier. But we are. To be truly mated we have to be mated on four levels: physical, emotional, mental and spiritual levels. This is difficult. A person, especially when he has not matured inside, may be attracted to another individual physically and emotionally, and yet have no understanding of the other person's needs and nature. If those involved are inwardly asleep the attraction is usually on the physical and emotional levels. As yet, the mental and spiritual levels are not developed. The persons married. When the physical attraction is satiated and the emotions die down, they are often unhappy for they have little in common intellectually or spiritually. As time goes on one of them may developed these aspects of his being as he or she matures. The partner, having no yearning for growth in mind and spirit, resents the partner's desire for this growth. So he or she is frightened and afraid of loss, is angered and does everything he can to hold the other person back. People may be attracted to each other because they are stimulated by each other on the mind level. Mind attractions do stimulate but they do not completely unite two people. It is never "head to head" that unites, but "heart to heart." It is the heart that is the unifying force.

When one out of two marriages ends in divorce there must be a reason. Mating is not a matter of bodies merging or of emotional titillation. There must be a meeting of the minds as well as an understanding of spiritual ideals. If the first merging is on the physical level the union is usually a karmic one and represents a lesson brought over from another life to be worked out. If it starts on the level of spiritual ideals and works down through the mental and emotional levels, it is a cosmic tie that is really blessed. There may be difficulties on the personality level, but if the two involved go together to the real

Self within them both, they will be given guidance as to how to work out the problems they encounter.

Many young people in the world today think sexual freedom and promiscuity are their divine right and there will be no dues to pay. However, there will be. They do have the right to do as they please, but there is nothing divine about it. Every physical union creates a vortex of energy that swirls up the levels or down to lower levels, depending on whether it is a loving act or a lustful one. There are consequences in mating that are in need of recognition. Every union creates a third force. Symbolically, a child has been created on the psychic level although it may not result in a child in the outer world. The creative power of God is involved, and the use or abuse of that force will bind the two souls together through more than one lifetime. Can you imagine what kind of a thought-form lust creates on the psychic level. An animal like element goes forth seeking whomever it can fasten on and devour. A true union of souls is a sacrament and creates beauty and harmony that goes forth to bless and heal.

When I first began my counseling, I wanted an answer to this love business. I could not believe that mating could be a dire sin if it was not legalized. Yet it could bring so much sorrow and pain in its wake. In a deep meditation this answer came: There are two questions we have to answer if mating is to incur no negative karma. Our only judge and our only jury is our own inner Self. If we stand before that High Self and can answer these two questions rightly, we need have no concern:

"Are we truly loving?"

"Does it hurt anyone?"

It is many years since I received that guidance. The years that have passed have shown me the wisdom of this teaching.

The reasons for so many problems are often tied up with experiences of our past lifetimes. Some of us come into this life with very little

61

capital in our spiritual bankbooks as far as love is concerned. We love and are not loved in return. Until we have capital in our love banks, how are we going to draw love out? The blueprint we call the horoscope shows what we have, or do not have, in our love bank. If we have failed to be loving in other lives, how can we get love from others? So many times, people have said to me, "If I had someone to love I could be a very loving person." It does not work that way. Love is a radiating force, a potent energy that comes from an individual and attracts to itself its own kind of energy. Until we radiate love to all those in our orbit, we will not attract that same energy to us. Yes, I know. You will see many people who are apparently unloving, yet they have love in their lives. They are the souls who came into this life with a goodly amount of capital in their love bank. It is earned increment from other lifetimes. If they overdraw their account by accepting love and fail to be loving they are drawing out their capital. They can end in bankruptcy. The individual that may have had little to start with in the beginning may fill up his love bank by loving. He may end up with lot his love capital overflowing.

Some of us have love for a season and then it departs. Others have it much longer. In God's garden of love there are annuals and perennials. Is an annual less beautiful because it blossoms for a season? We cannot make a perennial out of an annual, or an annual out of a perennial. Both have their place. No flowers, whether annuals or perennials, can grow without care. They need sunshine and rain, and air in which to breathe. The garden has to be weeded constantly to keep it from being choked by weeds. Love is like a garden. If we neglect it and it dies whose fault is it? Ours, of course. Half of the grief at loss is the guilt feeling engendered because love was not appreciated until it was too late.

When a relationship is broken, long after the head repudiates the relationship, the individuals concerned are not free. The symbolic child on the psychic level has to die from malnutrition before there is freedom. If we understand this truth it will help us to get through that lonely and difficult time after the loss of someone to whom we have been tied. The busier we keep, and the less we feed that memory through our thinking and feeling, the sooner the necessary healing will come. Nature and time bring healing. Our hangup can be impatience. We cannot change the past but today is in our hands. The future will depend on our attitude and consciousness today. Today is all we have. Fill it with loving and loving the future is assured. Love comes, many times love goes, but love never leaves. Love is an energy. Use it or abuse it, the choice is always ours. Growth comes from being loving, not from being loved.

CHAPTER X

HEALING VS. DISEASE

With the dawning of the Aquarian Age we are rediscovering an ancient forgotten truth that there is a relationship between a person and the physical body in which he lives. Psychosomatic medicine is now a recognized fact of medical practice. This has not always been believed. Today the change is the direction of attempting to discover and treat the underlying causes of ill health. Physicians have been finding that the cause lies much deeper than has hitherto been supposed. The roots of ill health lie in the mental and emotional patterns of the individual. Ill health does not start in the physical body, although frequently that is where the trouble manifests. Individual feelings and attitudes mold the body. The body does not mold the mind and feelings. A very simple example is what happens when a person has had an emotional shock. His face turns white. When a person is very embarrassed what happens? His face turns red and blood rushes to his cheeks. It was the thoughts and feelings that caused the body to react.

Every disease in the physical body starts first in our thoughts and feelings before it manifests in our physical bodies. There is a definite relationship between the person in the body and the type of illness attracted. If the individual in the body changes his patterns of behavior and his attitudes, he can overcome any illness. There is no disease on this planet that has not been cured, but there are many people who have not been healed. Only when the inner causes of the illness are eradicated does the healing take place.

So many of us do not know what we are doing to our bodies when we fill ourselves with negative thoughts and feelings. We are putting toxins into our minds that will have to go into our bodies for clearance. We know what physical infections can do. How about mental and emotional infections? They are just as deadly. There is waste matter in our thoughts and feelings that must be eliminated, as well as in our physical bodies. Illness is often the result of faulty elimination on the psychological levels. There are emotional and mental kinds of constipation as well as the physical kind. Even in the world of appearance we have to be careful not to pick up infections from other people. Have you ever been in a situation where there were "vibes" from people that were exceedingly negative? You began to feel depressed and decided you must leave. If you had wrapped yourself – and the other – in your Robe of Light, using your creative imagination to do so, and had purposely and inwardly let Light and Love flow through you, you could have been an agent of healing and lifted the vibration to a higher level.

As an astrological counselor, and one very interested in medical astrology, I came to certain conclusions that were verified by a physician, and a spiritual healer, as well as by a clairvoyant who had the ability to see the inner bodies and diagnose diseases before they appeared on the physical level. By change of attitude, the disease could be prevented from appearing on the outer levels. In our research we found out the inner reasons for outer diseases. Investigation showed that the people who suffer from arthritis are very fixed in their opinions and extremely stubborn. They are good people but, without realizing it, are also very self-righteous. Often they get locked in their antagonisms because they want to be good and not hurt people. They have been told since childhood that they should be well behaved and not express their real feelings. So they lock up their emotions and their joins in the physical body as well.

At the Peter Bent Brigham Hospital in Boston they specialize in treating arthritic patients. In a paper written by a psychiatrist on the staff, he stated there was a definite type of personality that suffered from arthritis. It was the type I have described. A doctor who specialized in joint diseases and arthritic conditions told me that in all his practice he never had an alcoholic patient. He said their bodies are always loose and they flow. They do not tighten up, though everyone around them may! Their livers may be, and usually are, affected, but not their joints and, as a rule, they never attract arthritis.

Diabetes was found to be caused by bitterness. The opposite to bitterness is sweetness. Sugar has always been a symbol of sweetness and it is a sugar imbalance in the body that causes diabetes. I remember well a girl who came to me for counseling. After I had drawn up her astrological chart, I saw that she was a very bitter person and had all the birthchart constants for diabetes. This was the conversation:

"You are a very bitter person, aren't you?"

"Yes, I am."

"And you have diabetes?"

"Yes, but what has that to do with my diabetes?"

"Everything."

We talked about it. She came to our meditation and healing group and changed her old attitudes. The diabetes disappeared.

Heart trouble is related with a person's feeling of not being loved or not achieving his drive for significance in this life. This does not mean that love is not all around him or that he has not had great achievement. However, he does not feel it, if he has not been nourished by it. I made this statement during a lecture I was giving one night at a Women's Club. A woman challenged my statement saying, "My husband died of heart trouble and he was dearly loved." I said, "A person could be sitting at a banquet table loaded with food.

If he was unable to reach for it, take it in and digest it, he could starve, couldn't he?" It is not how much a person is loved, but how much can he feel it, and thus know inwardly that he is loved.

Those who have studied astrology and know the correlation between the signs and the parts of the body, know Capricorn rules the knees, and false pride and unwillingness to bend are the forerunners of trouble with the knees. Back trouble and difficulties in the spine do not begin with the body. The spine gives us the ability to stand erect and is the outer symbol of the will to be. Have you known anyone with back trouble who was not self-willed? It is not that will wrong. we cannot move forward without it. But it is how we use that will that decides the issue. Leo rules the spine and the will.

The kidneys are the purifiers of the body. The sign Libra rules the kidneys in the body. In astrology we find Libra correlate with relationships, particularly in marriage or unions. This puzzled me when I was studying astrology. Why should it be so? Because as the kidneys are the purifiers of the bloodstream, so marriage and unions are the purifiers of our personalities. Where others are involved we have to learn cooperation and the art of compromise, otherwise we have no relationships.

Feet have always been the symbol of understanding. Difficulties with the feet are the outer manifestation of inner lack of understanding. When we dream about feet or shoes (covering our feet) our subconscious self is trying to tell us something. When Jesus washed his disciples' feet it was the symbol of washing clean their understanding. Have you ever been in the Bowery and seeing the souls who have given up and lost their incentive to live? They shuffle along and their walk tells a story about their loss of understanding.

The forerunners of cancer can be deep seated resentment, anger and fear. A group of cells in the body decide they want nothing to do with other cells. So they huddled together and start preying on the other

68

cells, not knowing that they are finishing themselves off. Is not war a planetary cancer caused by fear and greed?

Every function of the body repeats itself on another level. The food for our psychological body (our mind and emotions) is experience. In order to be nourished on that level we first have to accept (swallow) the experience. Then we must go through the processes of absorption, assimilation and elimination. Sometimes it is very difficult for us to believe it, but only that which we need for our growth and development comes to us. If we do not digest the experience, or if we fail to assimilate it or to eliminate what is not needed, we can become ill. There is constipation of the mental and emotional bodies, just as truly as we can have toxins in our physical bodies because of improper elimination. When we are bitter, resentful and unforgiving we are filling our minds and emotions with poisons that, sooner or later, will become part of the physical body.

If, in ignorance, we create these conditions, then through understanding we can redeem them. An unusual clairvoyant friend told me that just as we have scars on our bodies if a physical wound is a deep one, so we have scars on our astral bodies if we have been deeply wounded in our emotions. She could look at a person and tell how many times there had been a deep emotional wound in that person's life. Wounds heal, but if they are deep, the scars remain. She could see scar tissue in the mental body, and said it was caused by prejudices and crystallized opinions. Those crystallized clusters interfered with a free flow of energy in the mind just as scar tissue in the physical body can interfere with the flow of vitality in the body. Depression, as seen clairvoyantly, shuts off the flow of vitality into the physical body. If continued, ill health is the result.

There is no illness that cannot be cured. The spirit in each and every one of us has power to heal any condition or dis-ease or lack of harmony of any kind. Not every person can be healed, for many reasons. Some people do not want to be healed. They think they do, but subconsciously they do not. If they were healed, it might mean they would have to face responsibilities they do not want to face. Others are punishing themselves for some guilt, real or unreal, that is held on the subconscious levels. Others hold the power over their family through sickness. Sometimes it is unfinished business from a past life and the soul chooses to work out its debt through sickness.

When a child is suffering from a disease, so often people say, why should an innocent child have to suffer? There is no innocence on earth. The body is new, but the soul in the body has been in and out of many bodies. And the soul knows on the higher levels exactly why that particular experience is needed. All hereditary and congenital diseases are the results of actions performed in past lives. Clairvoyant investigation has shown this fact to be true. One young man had a blind grandmother for whom he had to care. She dominated his life completely for she was helpless and there were no other relatives. In looking into his akashic records, they showed that he had been a cruel and domineering ruler of a Middle Eastern tribe. In that lifetime, when he was in an angry mood, he would have slaves whipped or their eyes put out, just to satisfy his whims. The grandmother was a slave to whom this had happened. Her hatred of him and his cruelty brought them back together again. In this life he has to be her eyes as well as being dominated as he once dominated others.

What is the source of health in the body? Vitality. The Easterner calls it prana. It flows into the threefold personality from inner and higher levels. When we become rigid and resistant to new ideas, we limit the flow of the vitality into the mind. Prejudice and intolerance cut off the flow of life force. In the emotional body it is worry, fear and depression that shut off the circulation of life force. In astrology the planets (energy points) are correlated with the glandular system. Each ductless gland is an outer aspect of a psychic center that the

Eastern teachers call a Chakra. It is through those centers that vitality flows from the etheric level into the physical body.

Science has proven that plants respond to love as well as to the opposite quality of hate. How about the cells in our physical bodies? Everyone thrives on love and appreciation. Have you ever thanked your physical body for all it does for you? Every cell has an intelligence of its own. Bless your body, talk to it lovingly, and know that all healing, just as all lack of harmony (disease) starts from within. All the power to heal lies in the Self.

When asking for a healing, or praying for someone who needs healing, never dwell on the disease or difficulty. See the healing accomplished. Energy follows thought. It is better not to pray than to pray and hold the disease in your consciousness. It will increase the difficulty rather than heal it.

Today, with the veils between the dimensions becoming thinner, the ability to be a healer or to be healed is greater than it ever was.

CHAPTER XI

THE DIS-EASE CALLED ALCOHOLISM

Our world 'out there,' the world we call the world of appearance, is a projection of our consciousness. This is unknown to us until we understand the universal laws that rule our planet. We wonder why some people are born into certain families where someone has a problem involving alcohol. Perhaps a marriage partner is an alcoholic. If we have been an alcoholic in a past life, we can be sure that we will not be so in our next lifetime. When we leave the body and go Home, we survey the life that we have left behind us. We see the damage we have done with the abuse of alcohol to our minds and bodies, as well as the damage we have done to others in our environment.

Having learned through experience, when we go back to earth, we will not fall into that trap again. Half of the lesson has been learned. There will be no desire to over-indulge in that habit again. The other half of the lesson is receiving and accepting from others that treatment which we gave them. On the inner levels before we come into incarnation, we as souls will choose a family or a marriage where we will have a chance to pay our dues. We will be treated by others as we once treated others. Space is curved. There is no such thing as a straight line in the universe. Everything must return to its source. What we meet in the outer world is ourselves as we once were.

It is the Inner Self that sends down a personality saying: "Go down there into a family where you will be tuned to the vibrations you once sent out. Feel the hurt and anguish you caused to others. Experience the pain and suffering you once caused others to feel. Accept the lesson without anger or resentment so that you will be forever free of the lessons you needed to learn. By helping, and not condemning the one who is afflicted as you once were you will balance the karmic scales. You will be free and will come under the law of grace (God's Will) instead of the karmic pattern (self-will).

Alcoholism is a disease that stems from the psychological body. The individual feels inadequate and unequipped to face life without the false courage that liquor provides. It is well to remember that when a person is intoxicated, he or she is not functioning on the conscious level where reason and logic can be used. He is functioning on the subconscious level where logic and reason are nonexistent. It is useless to argue or reason with an individual when he is intoxicated. He is tuned into the subconscious (psychic) levels and knows what you are feeling and thinking. If you are angry and resentful, the intoxicated person knows that you are, he will return your thoughts and feelings threefold. This is the time the individual can be helped the most. If you think inwardly in the right manner the message will be received. Tell him (without opening your mouth) how God loves him, how worthwhile he is, bless him and ask that he might be healed of all the obstructions that have shut him off from knowing these truths. They are truths whether or not he, or you, know it. Feel God's love and compassion wrapping him close. Never mind whether you like him or not. That does not really matter. Liking is something the outer self has to earn. Love is God in action. Get your own unlit self, the personality out of the way. Then you can be a channel of God's Love and Power.

For some years I had a studio in a Boston hotel where I did counseling and had classes in personality integration. One evening one of my students and I went down to the restaurant connected to the hotel to have an early dinner before class began. At the other end of the restaurant was a bar. When we sat down, we could hear a great commotion at the other end of the restaurant. It was quite a distance from where we were sitting. On one of the stools in front of the bar was a woman who was about sixty years of age. She was very drunk. The bartender was refusing to sell her anymore liquor. The language that was issuing from her mouth was picturesque to say the least. She was very angry. I looked at my student and said: 'Let's go to work.' We tuned in and asked that she might feel God's love and peace all around her, and that she would know she was loved.

All of a sudden, she swung around on the stool and looked in our direction. She waved, got down from her stool, and weaved her unsteady way to where we were sitting. She sat down and we talked lovingly to her. It was desultory conversation but inwardly we were asking God to bless her and heal her. We found out she was staying in the hotel. After a while I said: "Don't you think it would be a good idea to go up to your room and have a rest before dinner? You will feel better." Her answer, as she rose on her still unsteady underpinnings, was: "I will do it for you but I won't do it for that --- of a ----- at the bar."

After she left the bartender came over. This was the conversation:

"Do you know that woman?"

"No, we never saw her before."

"How did you get her out of here?"

"We loved her."

"You WHAT?"

"We simply loved her."

"Well, I have been a bartender here for fifteen years. I have tried every method I know to get rid of drunks, short of calling the police. That's a new one and I saw it work. Maybe the next time I will try your way."

He went back to the bar, shaking his head and obviously trying to figure out what had happened.

In healing work, alcoholics are easy patients to work with. This may be hard to believe unless you have used the technique yourself. Some years ago, Jane Revere Burke, a powerful healing channel, had a prayer and healing group in Boston. We met once a week at her home. One of our projects had to do with healing for Alcoholics. Seven of us agreed to take someone we knew who was afflicted with this disease. We promised to put them in God's healing Light three times a day and to talk to their subconscious minds before we went to sleep at night. Within four months each one had stopped his drinking. It was done secretly so no one, except the seven of us, knew what we were doing. One man, a brilliant reporter on one of the daily newspapers, had been drinking heavily for twenty-five years. The man who had been praying for him met him on the street about four months after we had begun our work. The man looked wonderful. He told the gentleman who had been praying for him that he had stopped drinking and was feeling great. "How come you decided to stop after all these years?" "I don't know. I woke up one morning knowing I would never take another drink. I haven't taken a drink since that morning and I don't think I will ever take another drink." Years have passed and he hasn't. A skeptic might have said we were wasting our time. But each of those for whom we prayed stopped drinking.

One day I was riding on a streetcar. A man got on who was very strongly under the influence of alcohol. He was well dressed and aristocratic in manner. I had the feeling that this was not his usual behavior. There were no empty seats, so he stood, holding a strap, in front of two women. Their disgust and censoriousness showed in their faces. Inwardly I went to my High Self and asked that he be blessed and helped. He moved down the car and stood in front of me. He was pleasant and made some comments about the weather. We talked until he came to his stop. As he moved to go out of the car he turned and said, "Lady, will you pray for me?" I smiled and said, friend, "I already have. God bless you."

Why do you suppose we call alcohol "spirits"? Why are bars and cocktail lounges dimly lit with the color red so dominant in many of them? Why do these places do their greatest volume of business at the time of the full moon? I asked a cocktail lounge owner why she didn't put up the shades and let the sunlight in. "If I did, I would lose all my business. People would not come in." She was the person who told me she never had to look at the calendar. She always knew when the moon was full. Think about the reason for these facts. Have you ever seen a complete change of personality when a person has had too much alcohol? Have people told you they could not remember anything they did or what happened to them when they were very drunk? They are telling the truth. Have you ever looked in the eyes of an inebriated person and seen someone else looking through those eyes? You could have had that experience and wondered about it.

There are answers. But those completely asleep in matter never ask the questions that would give them the answers. When a person drinks to excess he opens himself to the lower levels of the psychic (astral) plane. Liquor is rightly called "spirits." There is a protective web around each of us that is between the physical body and the psychic body. Excessive use of liquor or drugs destroys that web and leaves the individual open to invasion of entities who haunt those dim-lit places to get the fumes of the alcohol that the person is drinking. The entities are earthbound and still have the craving they cannot satisfy on their own. The color red and the dimly lit places helped them to enter. If we could see psychically what goes on in dimly lit lounges or bars we would not want to go in them and if we did we would protect ourselves psychically.

Some years ago, I was praying for a friend of mine whom I will call Jim. He was loved by all who knew him, and he was an alcoholic. No one knew I was praying for him. One day I took another friend of mine to see a very wonderful clairvoyant, whom I felt could help my friend. I was going to do some shopping while the interview was taking place. As I was going out the door the clairvoyant called me back.

"Isabel, are you praying for a fellow named Jim who is alcoholic?"

"Yes, I am."

"Stop praying for him and pray for his Aunt Fanny. She died an alcoholic and is obsessing him."

I knew none of Jim's relatives. The next time I saw Jim I asked if he had an aunt Fanny who was out of the body. He said, "Yes, but how do you know?" "Was she an alcoholic?" I asked. He said she was and wanted to know why I asked this. "Do you see her or feel her around you when you have taken too much liquor?" His answer was "How do you know that I do? You must be psychic or something!" I changed the subject and said no more about it. From then on I prayed for his Aunt Fanny and asked that she be released. Jim stop drinking, joined the AA and became a powerful helper and healer to others who were afflicted with that dis-ease.

CHAPTER XII

DEATH – THE OTHER SIDE OF LIFE

One of the most certain things in a world of uncertainties is that every one of us has to leave the world we live in sooner or later. So many people will not allow themselves to think about or discuss that fact. On the earth plane, when we are going to take a trip to a foreign country, we want to know what the place is like, the climate, the people and the terrain. We learn as much as we can before we go there. Many people die many times in their minds through fear. Yet these same people are not afraid to go to sleep at night. As Michael said, "The only difference between sleep and death is that when a person dies he forgets to come back here in the morning." While our bodies sleep we are on the next dimension and are with our loved ones who are living there. To a great extent the fear of death has been engendered by the dogma and the orthodoxy of many of the religious creeds and teachings, especially in the Western world.

When we are born and come into a new body our first action is a protest. We cry. Who wants to be confined in that small body once again and have to live in it until it grows big enough to use as a vehicle on the earthplane? When it is our time to leave our bodies, other people do the crying. When we leave the inner planes of consciousness to come into earth manifestation, those we leave behind say, "There they go." Those waiting to greet us here say, "Here they come." When we leave here to go back home those here say, "They are gone," but those waiting for us on the other side say, "Here they are." Then what is death, and what is life? Change there is and change there must be. There is no death. It is merely a change of dimension. When we take off the clothes we are wearing, we are the same individuals. If we take off the garment of flesh we are living in here, we are still the same. Dying doesn't change anything except our area of action. Whatever we are here we will be in the next dimension. So many people ask, "Will I know my loved ones there?" Of course they will. The outer body is a replica of the body of the next dimension. It will be a more refined and a healthier body. There is no sickness there, and no old age. Sometimes we bring back from sleep memories of seeing our loved ones who have gone on ahead. Be sure it is an authentic experience if you see them young and vital.

Recently a student of mine had an example of this truth. Her mother had been sick a long time, and unable to use her legs for a number of years. Finally, the test and trial was over, and the mother left the body. Two weeks later Rose had a very vivid dram that she knew was more than a dream. Her mother came to her, young and vital and full of joy. "Look, Rose, I can walk. I am well again." Rose shared her joy for she knew all was very, very well with her mother.

One Saturday morning in the springtime of 1951 my mother, seventy years old, was up early baking bread and beans for Saturday supper. As my sister and mother were having breakfast this conversation took place: "Mary, prepare yourself, for it is time for me to leave the body." (Mary had always been frightened of anyone she loved dying.)

"What do you mean, Mother? Except for your arthritis you are in good health. What makes you say such a thing?"

"Last night when I was sleeping John came to me and said, 'Come on, Ma. We're waiting for you. You are overdue. Come on.' He beckoned me and said, 'Get going.'"

John, her oldest and most adored son, had died in 1921 as a result of poison gas in the first world war. He went to France at 16 and was 20 years old when he left the body. It was the hardest cross she had to face in this lifetime.

Mary was upset. "Oh, Mother, that was only a dream."

"No, Mary, it was not a dream."

The day went on as usual until four o'clock in the afternoon. Mother had a sudden heart attack and within fifteen minutes was on her way to be with her loved ones.

Our loved ones on the inner dimension know when we are joining them. Love never loses its own. Our bodies may be forced apart for a little while, but we find each other again. It is love for each other that creates the drawing power. The ties that bind us from life to life are love and hate. Love enough and we find each other whether in the body or out of it. If we hate anyone or have failed to be loving, we will not be with them on the inner levels but when we come back to earth, we will be drawn into their orbit to work out the unfinished lesson. When I asked my Initiate teacher what the inner reason was for Siamese twins, I received this reply: "They are the result of hatred to the 'nth degree. It is the result of intense hatred for each other over many, many lifetimes." What a price to pay! Never a moment to be alone and to be your own private person. Not far from where I grew up there were sisters, Siamese twins, who were bound together. I felt so badly for them. It was difficult to understand why they had such a cross to bear. At that time, I did not know that we fashion our own crosses which we have to assume and carry.

Leaving the body does not change anything except the dimension on which we are functioning. The outer vehicle is a replica of the inner body so we will recognize each other when we meet. There is no age or sickness on the other side of life. I have seen two friends of mine after they left their bodies. Both of them had been sick a long time before they left. I was puzzled for they were both in rest homes with loving care surrounding them. I asked, "If there is no pain or sickness there, why should this be?" The answer came. "Consciousness IS the only reality. They had the consciousness of sickness deeply embedded in their emotions. So they needed to rest and recuperate from the long held feeling of sickness although they had no pain and were no longer sick."

Where do we go when we leave the body in sleep? We go to the same dimension that we go to when we leave this particular body for good. This is why it is difficult for some people to accept the fact, when they die (as we use the word), that they have left the body. They feel fully alive and they feel normal. If they stay around the earthplane, as some do for a little while, they wonder why people around them will not talk to them. If the transition has been sudden and unexpected it is difficult for them to realize what has happened. Now I know why some orthodox religions pray that the soul be delivered from a sudden death. In one case, an individual had left the body unexpectedly and he did not know he was dead. He could not understand why his family would not talk to him. However, he was able to reach my consciousness and I had to convince him he had left his body before he would accept the fact that he was not in the same body he had been in the day before.

The physical body is but the castoff garment. Whenever we stand in front of a body in a casket, we should talk mentally to the person who has left. Many times, he or she is standing beside you. I have had the experience of seeing the casket in the aisle in front of the altar, with people filing by it, while the person whose body it once was would be standing beside me watching the whole procedure. Sometimes the comments they make are very amusing. We do not lose our sense of humor (if we had one) when we are out of the body. As you talk to the person mentally, explain to him what has happened. This is particularly important if the departure has been a sudden one. You will get an inner verification that you have reached the person even though you do not see him physically. How can you see him if he is not in the physical body?

Dying is easy. It is living in the densest, coarsest matter of all that is difficult. Many of us feel that the earth plane is the hell that evangelists rant about. What is hell? It is the absence of Love and Light. It is not a place. It is a state of consciousness. If we can bring Love and Light into expression here on the earth planet, we can have heaven right here and we will take it with us when we leave.

Why do we fear death? It has happened to us many times. We are forever. Though we may put on many bodies, the Self in the body has the same identify through all time and space. We change in consciousness through the experiences and experiments of learning how to live and how to love. But we are the same self. When we have learned how to love and live we are truly free, free to go to higher and happier conditions. Some there are who have earned that freedom but who choose, as they stand at the gate to their paradise, to take a very special vow seven times over: "Never shall I enter the door of my paradise until the last one of God's children has come home." So back to the earth they come. Can you imagine what that vow entails? They are willing to forego the heaven they have earned and to bind themselves for untold ages to the densest and coarsest of all the levels. Few can conceive the magnitude of their Love and the deep meaning of that vow.

The soul, not the personality, chooses the time to withdraw from the body. Just as it chooses the time it will enter the body, it chooses the time it will leave. In spite of what some Orthodox religions imply, there is no sin when a person decides he has had enough and commits what the world calls suicide. The person that owns the body has the right. It is foolish, however, for when he gets into the inner dimension, he realizes he has "copped out" on an experience *he* chose for his own

83

growth and development. He knows that after a rest he must come back to earth and go through the experience again and pass the test.

Let me share an experience that proves it is not a sin. For many years we have had a meditation and healing group every week. One night a member came in just as we were starting our healing meditation. She said, "Will you put Mr. Stevens into the meditation tonight?"

I nodded. We always have had a time of silence in a deepening of consciousness before names are mentioned for the healing. When it came time and I mentioned Mr. Stevens, I had a very deep feeling of loneliness, a loneliness that was almost too much to bear.

I said, "I don't know what the matter is with Mr. Stevens, but I know he needs to feel God's love all around him. And I know he needs to know that he does not have to feel so alone."

After the meeting, I asked Dorothy what was the matter with him. "His body was found in the river this morning. He lost his wife two years ago and he couldn't stand the loneliness."

For four weeks after that night at every meditation I'd say, "Let's not forget Mr. Stevens."

The fourth week, a person who had not come to the meditation before came with a friend who was a regular participant. After the meeting and during refreshment time the stranger came up and said, "Usually I do not tell people, but I am clairvoyant. Your friend, Mr. Stevens, was here tonight and gave me a message for you. Before I give you the message, I would like to describe his appearance so you could verify that it was he."

Since I had never seen Mr. Stevens, I called Dorothy over to listen. The description was accurate. This was the message: "Tell them I am all right. Their prayers have brought me into the light. Tell them that in gratitude for what they have done for me, every time they meet, I shall be with them, adding my prayers for others to their petitions for healing."

God is Love, was Love, always will be Love. He does not punish us. There is no condemnation where there is Love. How long before that realization will come to each and every one of us? If we make mistakes, we have the opportunity to rectify them. There is no death. What happens is only a change of place and a new body and a new chance. When we shut our eyes on the earth plane, we open them on the next dimension. Everyone who has had a glimpse of that dimension bears witness to its beauty and its glorious freedom from pain or lack of any kind.

We have the body now which we will live in on the next dimension. We cannot see it because it is made of ether. It looks the same as our physical bodies although it is made of more refined matter. It interpenetrates the physical body as water fills a sponge. Some people with inner vision can see it. While we are awake the two bodies remain together but when we sleep, we slip into the inner body so that our physical bodies can be recharged and energized. This also happens when we take an anesthetic or a knocked unconscious. All feeling and sensation is in the etheric or astral body.

I had a friend who was one of the first women surgeons to graduate from Massachusetts General Hospital. She was an ear, nose and throat specialists who had clairvoyant vision, although she never discussed it with her intimate friends. Dr. K. Always knew when a group was praying for someone being operated on for there would be a band of healing angels there. It did not matter which church or sect the person belonged to. Many times, Dr. K. would be guided through the operation by healing angels. One morning she was doing a very difficult mastoid operation. It was in the days before penicillin was discovered.

She had prayed for guidance and, as she started, she saw a healing angel standing by her side. Suddenly she saw the angel beckon to the anesthetist and the impression came very strongly to alert him and break her scrub. At that moment the patient's heart failed, but the quick action of the three in that room helped her, and her heart started functioning again.

Just as there are angels at every birth and angels of healing present in crises (*when* they are invited in), so there are angels of death who come and take our loved ones over to the other side of life. There is another phenomenon that a sensitive experiences, that puzzled me until I found out what it meant. Towards the end of living on this plane the individual changes. The deeper, sweeter calmer more loving self is operating and there is a light around that person that is more sensed than scene. He looks younger. It always startles me to see it for I know, even though the individual may appear very healthy, that he is getting ready to leave. Recently I came across a book that gave me the answer. It seems that when the soul is ready for transition, the lower self leaves for it cannot go into that next dimension. The soul — the abiding reality in us all — drops off the lower elements and its real beauty shines forth. In Germany they called the lower self the "doppelganger."

We do not die. After we leave this dimension we live in the next plane. We are attached to our physical bodies by a silver cord. Do you remember an old hymn that said, "Someday the silver cord shall break, and I no more as now shall see." Death is the cutting of that silver cord that ties us to the body.

Where is the next dimension? Here, surrounding us. It is another wavelength. If we were able to tune our instruments to that wavelength, we would see our loved ones, know what they were doing, and know what that dimension was like. A few people are able to do this.

If we knew how very beautiful conditions are on that other side of life, it would be difficult for us to stay here. Perhaps that is why we do not know until we are willing to go God's way and accept the learning and the discipline life brings us here on the earth plane. On the other side of life there is no need for money. It is an unknown commodity on that other level. The dimension is a thought-built world. You can have anything you want if you can visualize it. Thought creates. Those who have learned to control their thoughts through concentration and meditation will be ahead of the rest who are not able to concentrate. For many years' metaphysicians have been saying, "If you want something, visualize it and hold the thought, and you will draw it to you." This is a cosmic law that works on all levels or dimensions. What we are able to think of clearly, we can have here as well as there. Due to the inertia of physical matter, the results work more slowly here. On the next dimension the result is simultaneous with the thought.

There is no marriage or family as we know it here. Love there is and always will be, and we will be drawn to our loved ones. Whatever the relationship is here, we shall still be related, but not as wife, husband, brother or sister. We will all be one family there and those on similar wavelengths will be drawn together. If we had yearnings and desires for artistic, intellectual or cultural achievements here that we were unable to satisfy, we will be able to attain them there. A spiritual teacher of mine started painting when she was eighty years old. she made the comment one day that she was starting something that she would continue on the other side and had enough time — if not here, then there — to achieve her heart's desire. It is never too late to start something here that can be continued when we step out of our overcoats of skin. There are classrooms and instructors there, and many here have wakened in the morning knowing they have been instructed while their bodies slept. As we become more conscious of ourselves as souls, we will remember more and more of what we have been taught during the sleeping hours.

The person who finds it difficult to adjust after leaving the body is the materialist. He has invested all his energies on the physical level, and he is stranded in a world where material things have no meaning. This person is apt to be earthbound, for only the earthly things have meaning for him. He will be bored on the next dimension until he learns to be creative in a cultural way.

Some of the old ideas about funerals and visiting cemeteries will drop away in the new age that is coming in. Cremation will be considered more and more, not only because of the wastefulness of using land for cemeteries, but because it is the quickest and best way to return earth to earth. We are not our bodies. If we identify ourselves too closely with the body, the idea of cremation will horrify us. If we wear a garment and in time it wears out, do we bury it and erect a monument to it?

How beautiful it would be if, on the anniversary of a loved one's death, we did something loving, and act of giving, for someone in need on earth in the memory of our loved one. Our loved ones are not in the cemetery, and going there to grieve only hurts them. They live. They are not dead. We live in a house, but we are not the house. We live for a while in a body, but we are not the body.

Earth is a school. When we graduate, we take with us the education we receive through attending that school. Death is a graduation into a higher dimension. Rejoice, for the loved one is free. Prayers and loving thoughts are presents to those living on the next dimension. Our love for them creates a line of light between here and there. They are able to use it to think back to us and to visit us; often they are unseen, but we know that when they are strongly in our thoughts, they are beside us.

CHAPTER XIII

EARTHBOUND – HERE AND AFTER HERE

Only if we know that we live in a multi-dimensional world will we understand that we are not confined to the physical plane alone. Yet there are those who choose, sometimes unwittingly, to be confined to the earth plane even after their vehicle, the body, has been returned to the elements from which it came. Some of the church fathers, especially Jesuits, have performed exorcisms to release those who have been earthbound so they could go on to the place that has been prepared for them. The prayer of exorcism is little known and so beautiful. "Father, take this, your love child, from the far-flung shores of exile to Thy bright home in Heaven where you and the blessed Mother have prepared a place for him."

The majority of earthbound souls are not evil. Many times, they are confused or frightened. Sometimes they do not know they have left their body. Many I have encountered were brought up in a Godfearing (not God loving) religion and taught the doctrine of hellfire and a vengeful God who would punish them for their sins. Under those circumstances it is natural that they were afraid to leave the earth plane even though their bodies had gone to dust. It is understandable and very human. If we take off our bodies, we are the same person as when we were in the body. My first experience of this kind was one of the most illuminating I have ever had. Our teacher had taught us that while our body slept, we could use the time to serve our Master on the inner levels or to gain spiritual knowledge. We leave our body in what we call "sleep" so that the physical instrument can be recharged and reenergized. The real Self does not need sleep. If we cared to do so we could make this prayer: "Father, use me in Thy vineyard while my body sleeps or let me be taught of Thee." For months, I made that prayer. One night, within myself, I said, "Father, I have been saying this prayer for a long time. I really want to know if I am able to serve while my body sleeps, or am I being fooled?"

That night my asking was answered. I was very conscious of being in another dimension. It was one I did not like very much. There were uncomfortable colors there, a murky green and a rusty looking red. I thought, "I don't like these colors." Immediately, an answer came in thought language, "These are the only colors we know here." I knew intuitively that I was being guided by a teacher spirit. Though I did not see the spirit, I knew it was behind me. I felt strongly that it was my High Self but even to this day my outer mind cannot be sure. I was impressed to go down into what seemed to be a basement, where I saw a young man reclining on a divan. On the inner dimensions, speech is not necessary, for communication occurs through thought language. Our conversation began. He said,

"Will you help me?"

"That is why I have come."

"What is the matter?"

"I have been earthbound since the First World War. I do so want to be free."

Time on the other dimensions is very different from what it is on the earth plane. I was impressed to put my arm around him and to say the Lord's Prayer. As I said the prayer his body writhed and seemed to be in great pain. It was as though it was being shredded and pulled apart. I had such compassion for his suffering, but I knew it was absolutely necessary if he were to be free. As I finished the prayer the body fell limp in my arms. Something went "swoosh" upward. At the same moment I was awake in my bed with my heart thumping from the sudden return to my body. For the first time in this life, I understood the Love and Compassion of Christ. He feels our pain in our suffering, but he sees beyond it to the freedom that lies beyond the painful shredding that is necessary to set us free. Love stands by and, knowing the necessity for the pain, can let it be, for through it the soul is freed and goes higher.

Another experience that I had one night while my body slept was also enlightening. I was in the hold of a ship that was breaking apart on an ocean. There were three very frightened men there, but it seemed my service had to do with only one of them. I told him it was going to be all right and not to be frightened. As I communicated these thoughts to him, it seemed as if that part of the ship was being pulled rapidly out of the water and up onto the land. He was jubilant for his thought was "We're saved." We were standing before what appeared to be a courthouse, and a man was standing at the door. I looked at the man and thought "We are out of the body, aren't we?" He nodded. The man with me was to go into the courthouse to be judged. He was frightened. I knew he felt guilty, for there were sins of the flesh weighing on his consciousness. However, I also knew the sins were not of great importance, and that he would learn this fact. Inwardly I asked, "May I go in with him so he will not feel alone?" The assent came and I followed him in. I could not see the judge (interesting!) but we were in the courtroom. A proud, arrogant dowager type of woman, in mink and diamonds, was on the witness stand. She had been guilty of meanness and cruelty to her servants. She had used her wealth to glorify her own appetites while her servants had been hungry and very poor. Suddenly she was dressed in very poor clothes. She was stripped of all her jewels. In one hand she held three pennies. She protested vehemently, "You can't do this to me. Don't you know who I am?" A beautiful voice rang out "Even as ye have done it to the least of these my little ones you have done it unto me." The scene faded, and I was back in my bed. I had learned a great deal on that errand of service.

Not always is this kind of service accomplished while away from the body. There have been occasions when it has happened in full waking consciousness. Always there have been three people involved. One was a clairvoyant who would allow the entity to use her vehicle. A second person would act as an energy battery. Then, I, the third, would talk with the person in need of help.

The first time this happened was a surprise and utterly unexpected. Three of us were sitting in a garden in New Hampshire on a beautiful summer day. Suddenly my friend Miriam went into a trance and a very agitated voice spoke through her. the entity said he was a young man. He and his shipmates were drowned at the bottom of the sea in a submarine and they were drowning like rats. he said the submarine was the S. S. Squalus. It had gone down off the Provincetown coast 10 years before. In his consciousness he was living the experience over and over again. His name was bill, and he said they had closed off one of the compartments to try to prevent the sinking of the submarine. The men in the compartment were drowning. His pal Eddie was in there, and bill was agitated because he knew he and Eddie were also drowning. Inwardly I asked how I could help. The impression came to get his attention and his consciousness to tell him he was no longer down in the squalus but was free. I told him to listen to me and to take a deep breath of the fresh air all around him and he would know he was free. After reiterating it over and over again I caught his attention. he took the deep breath of fresh air and was free. Miriam opened her eyes and said, I guess I fell asleep. She had no consciousness of what had transpired, no knowledge that the three of us had made contact with Billy, and that he had been set free. After this experience understanding was given that if anyone leaves the body under great stress he can get caught in the experience. It is as and I was back in my bed. I had learned a great deal on that errand of service.

After this experience understanding was given that if anyone leaves the body under great stress, he can get caught in the experience. It is as though a lock jams, and the person cannot get away from the consciousness of that moment. There is a reason why some of the church rituals say, "From a sudden death, Oh Lord, deliver us." If those who lose loved ones through a sudden and unexpected death would talk mentally to those loved ones, to tell them what had actually happened, they could be of great help to those who have passed on. We are just as human two minutes after we leave the body as we have been before we leave it. In this Aquarian age death will no longer be a mystery and feared. We will know our loved ones continue to live. Proof that no one can deny will be available.

Personal experiences are frequently helpful. Rachel, a friend and student of mine, was married with two young children, and she lived in the next town. Like her mother, her children were very psychic. They kept telling Rachel they did not like to go up to their playroom on the third floor for there was a man up there. He never said anything, but his presence bothered them. Rachel had not been conscious of him and thought it was her children's imagination until a mutual friend came to visit. After Marie's first night in the house she called me and asked if she could visit with me. On questioning her, she said she felt the spirit of the man, much as the children described. He did not seem to sense her presence, but she felt him and found the experience disconcerting, and it made her nervous. Knowing that Rachel would understand, I suggested Marie tell her of her feelings. When she did, Rachel suggested that Marie and I come to her home that night to talk to the spirit to find out why he was there. I knew Rachel had the power to be clairvoyant, Marie could act as a battery, and I would be able to reach the man's consciousness by talking with him.

We were in the third-floor bedroom when the three of us sensed his presence, and Rachel saw him clairvoyantly. The following conversation took place between the spirit and myself:

"What is your name, and why are you here?"

"My name is Edward, and this is my house. What are *you* doing here?"

"What year do you think it is, Edward?"

"1937, of course." It was 1970.

After some questioning, Edward revealed he had lived in that house for a long while. He had not realized the passage of time, but he was afraid to leave the house. He did not want to go to Hell. He had done something terrible, and he was a frightened soul. He had lived in the house for many years. His children had grown up there and married and left home. His wife was an irritable and angry person who made life miserable for him. When she was in her sixties, she contracted cancer and was sick a long while. She became exceedingly demanding and difficult to please. As her disease progressed, he brought in a registered nurse to take care of her.

Edward fell in love with the nurse, for she was very loving, and Edward had been starved for affection. His wife took a long time to die, and near the end of her illness, Edward and the nurse gave her a larger dose of medication than was usual. The wife was pushed out of her body before she was ready to leave. After his wife was buried, the nurse became frightened, took off, and very quickly married someone else. Poor Edward. He was left without love and with a very heavy load of guilt to carry. About six months later, he died of a heart attack. He could not bear the idea of burning forever in the lake of fire or seeing his wife again, so he stayed on his on in his home. He listened very intently when I told him that God does not punish us for anything we do and that Love — and God is Love — does not judge or condemn. When I asked him if he had been a father he replied, "Yes."   Then

I said, "If your children did wrong would you bring them in Hell for it?"

He responded quickly, "Of course not. I loved them."

"Then credit God with at least that much sense. He would not condemn them either. Nor has he condemned you. He Was, Is an Always Will Be Love."

Edward replied, "Well, that makes more sense than anything I was ever taught about God. If I leave here and go on, will I have to see my wife over there?"

When I reassured him, he would not have to see her, he was very relieved. "In the dimension in which you will be, you will be connected only with those whom you love. When you come back to earth again, however, you will meet the person who was your wife again, in a new relationship, and be given the chance to make amends, either through service or suffering. You will be able to handle the debt you owe her, for the next time you will have more understanding because of the experience you had this time." I went on, "Who did you love the most when you were here on earth, Edward?"

"My mother," was his reply.

Knowing the goodness of God, I asked that the healing angels bring his mother, or an angel who would appear to be his mother, to take him Home. We all heard the response. We heard Edward's voice filled with joy saying, "Mother." He was gone. Another child of God had gone Home.

Another incident with an earthbound soul took place in Kingston, New Hampshire. The head of a psychical research group telephoned me one day to ask if I would help a family that was being bothered by a spirit. The children in the house could see a man in their bedroom, and he frightened them. The father said the idea was nonsense and insisted there were no such things as ghosts. One night, he was alone in the house with the children who were sleeping. A banging sound, so loud it drowned out the television set, came from the cellar. He went down the stairs to the cellar and looked around. No one was there. He went back upstairs and as soon as he sat down in the living room, the noise started again. He was so angry he yelled, "Stop it," and added to his cry a few descriptive oaths. The noise stopped.

It was the day after these events that I received the call requesting my help. Knowing it was necessary to have three people there who understand the phenomenon common I called two young friends who are priests and asked if they would help. I had trained them in the technique. I asked them to fast that day. I also fasted. Fasting releases energy that can be used effectively on the inner dimensions. Jack is clairvoyant and I knew he could allow the earthbound spirit to use him to communicate with us. The other priest could act as a battery. I could talk to the entity. Already, I had sensed the spirit was not malicious. He was trying to attract attention so someone would help him.

As soon as we sat down, we offered up a prayer that we might be of assistance. Jack went into a semi-trance, and the man who had been staying in the house used Jack's vocal cords. He told us he was looking for his wife, Laura. He had lived in that neighborhood one hundred years ago. He further explained, he had not been very kind to Laura, and had treated her meanly. He wanted to find Laura to ask her forgiveness. He was consumed with the same fear that Edward had expressed. He did not want to go to Hell. But he feared he would have to do so to pay for his meanness. When I explained to him that God was a loving Father who did not want him to wander on the earth plane but rather wanted him to come Home, he listened. I asked him if he was willing to go.

"Yes. Will you please come with me? I am afraid."

"Yes, take my hand." I took Jack's hand.

"See that beautiful Light in front of you. Let's go into that Light." In consciousness I went with him. Suddenly his voice rang out, "It's

Laura. She is holding out her arms and is loving me. Me? Oh, God, thank you." He was gone.

We do not lose our humaneness because we take off the overcoat that we call the body. When we allow life and all that life gives us to flow freely through us, we are free — here and there.

One woman would not go on after her death because of a desk she owned. (Actually, it owned her.) She wanted it to be given to a certain individual. It had been given to someone else. She was angry and determined not to leave the earth plane until the desk was in the hands of the person to whom she wanted it given. It took some persuasion to help her see, she was holding up her own progress.

Another, a man, loved his home so much he refused to leave it when he left his body. He was furious because someone else was living in his house. He did not know he could build an identical home on the next dimension. All he had to do was to think it — visualize it — and there it would be. Thoughts are things on the next plane as truly as they are manifested eventually here in the world of appearance.

CHAPTER XIV

LETTERS FROM A SON TO HIS MOTHER

These comments are messages written by Jack to his mother after he had given up his body and was on the other side of life.

"Our physical bodies are just the coverings for ourselves, so it does not matter what happens to them when we're finished with them. After my body was blown up, I had a much nicer one and that was all that was needed. Get rid of the idea that we in the spirit worlds are like shadowy bits of cloud floating in space. We are nothing of the kind. We are still men, with bodies, feelings, affections and intelligence. We are living ordered busy lives, but in different conditions and methods from life on your plane.

"Get rid of that horrible word 'ghosts.' It conveys an utterly wrong impression. The spiritual world is all around you, Mother, just like the material world, and someday you will be advanced enough to see it.

"All we are taught here is reflected on your plane. That means that the plans of good people for the benefits of others on earth originate here. It is the case with all good work on your plane, including the books authors write, and think they are their own composition, and the same with music, science and inventions.

"Everything on your earth is a reflection of life here, and this makes our world the real one and yours the shadowy one. Ideas and concepts are originated here and floated into the minds of receptive people on your plane. Two people may pick up our ideas or concepts at the same time and then spend years fighting over whose possession they are. That happened when two men, Morton and Jackson, picked up the concept of ether at the same time. They spent years fighting over who was the inventor, little realizing the true facts.

"My Master wants you to make known to others that prayers for the so-called dead are very important. The Catholic Church has not failed in that respect, though charging money for prayers is wrong. They have remembered the souls in the spirit world and recognized their continued conscious existence. Many people believe that the dead have no need of their prayers. They think that because they have the false idea that death makes an absolute change in the soul's character and personality. We are no different two minutes after we leave the body than we were before we dropped it off. If you are wearing an overcoat and discard it, are you any different? The body is the overcoat the soul wears while in a physical body.

"Souls here want their loved ones' thoughts and prayers more than I can express to you. Often, I have had this said to me; "My people have forgotten me. They never speak of me at home." Their sadness wrings my heart. What you have done for me, Mother, and for ever so many others, passes all description. Simply that you would talk about me as if I were still on earth has helped me so very much.

"Many of us spend much time in comforting those souls whose loneliness on their first entry into spirit life is made much worse by the attitudes of their people on earth. Prayers and loving thoughts are like presents to us here.

"As I told you, our life here is the reality and yours is the shadow. At the same time, the shadowy life on your earth is of the greatest importance. The ego is sent into the physical body to learn lessons that only earth life and conditions could teach. On the way he conducts himself during his earth life depends his state of advancement in the spiritual world. Our life here is real, just as full of duties and pleasures and educational advancement as life on your plane. There are schools of learning here, of all grades, and everyone can attend one or the other of them, if it is needed for their development.

"Nothing that I can tell you, Mother, of the love of Christ for souls on your plane can give you any real idea of the power of it. If you could imagine the most unselfish person you ever knew, and mix that up with all the kindness you can imagine, and add on to that the happiness of the happiest hearted person you can think of, you would get some idea of the Master's personality.

"People must not think of Him as grieving over the wickedness of people on the earth and being mildly and rather mournfully pleased when they make an effort to do what is right. Our Master is a strong Spirit, brimming over with kindness and love of laughter and happiness. The ordinary idea of Christ with a good many people is a rather effeminate one. This has come about through the confusion of the two distinct personalities, looking on the Master Christ and His faithful disciple Jesus of Nazareth, as one person. And then the pictures of Him do not give one the idea of a powerful personality. Always there is a marked suggestion of weakness and awful sorrow. Of course, the Master is grieved about the wickedness on earth, but he knows that it will all work out in the end, as it worked through so many thousands and thousands of years ago.

"The great disciple, Jesus, had not the full knowledge our Master had when they were working in Syria 2,000 years ago, but he knew a great deal more than appears in the Christian Bible. You know it is possible for some people on your plane to read the past clairvoyantly, and so they know a great deal more about him than the public generally. They know what a long and severe training he had before his mind and his body were ready for the habitation of our great

Master. He went to all sorts of schools in different parts of the world — in Egypt and India — until the time came for him to come back to Palestine, and the Master Christ came to begin His work in the body of Jesus.

"That entry took place when that other faithful worker, John, baptized whom he thought was Jesus, the son of Joseph. After that, the Master taught in Palestine for the three years recorded in the Bible, and then on the night of the betrayal by that poor soul, Judas, His work in the body of Jesus was finished. Jesus was killed. Our Master had left the body of his disciple Jesus before the crucifixion of the latter. It was a man who was killed, not the son of God. (This explained to me the meaning of what Jesus said on the cross: "My God, my God, why hast thou forsaken me?")

"After the crucifixion our Master materialized in the form of Jesus to ever so many people he had known on earth. Jesus came here to the spirit world to perfect his training. The Master Christ stayed on the earth after his servant had left the earth and taught in many countries. Jesus, the disciple, is a very high spirit now and very near to our Master. Mary, his mother, often comes to my part of the spirit world. She has the most lovely face you can imagine, Mother, and full of sympathy for all women. She was not many years on earth the last time, but she made the utmost use of her opportunities and loved God and all mankind; so there was no need for further earth life for her when her dearly loved son died, for the teaching of his Master.

"My Master wants people to be taught that they are wrong who say there is no such thing as a devil; there is not one devil but myriads of them, all seeking to do the utmost harm they can to people on the earth, on account of the hate they bear toward the Master Christ. Don't you think that if people realized this it would help them enormously to help Him. We think so here. He only smiles sadly when he is told how indignant we are for Him, but of course He is much too kind to blame anyone, but we know He is awfully pleased when He hears of anyone overcoming evil and the victory gained. Of course, my message will make people say, 'Why does not Almighty God destroy these evil powers if He is omnipotent?' Well, it is just this: if the evil were destroyed by God, the evolution of man on earth would stop dead. There would be no need to struggle with nothing to struggle against. Automatic goodness would be the result, which is not what Almighty God intends. His plan is that through endless trials and many failures, man at last obtains his final victory and stands before the great Ruler of all the worlds in all the purity, her beauty, and the strength of the Master Himself. A magnificent conception of the possibilities of the human ego, Mother, and certain of fulfillment no matter how long it takes.

"When the Master comes to earth again, which He will, one of the most important points of his teaching will be the meeting of friends who have loved each other with a very deep affection. Nothing binds people when they live here but love, and attraction, by reason of the same tastes, pleasures and ideas. Family ties do not exist just because they belonged to the same family on earth. If they loved each other, they will be together here. It means that no one is chained to uncomfortable relations because of earth ties.

"This is rather an urgent fact to press home to people, because we know here that the probability of being obliged to live with people whom you failed to love on earth, is a very great trouble to some folk. They need have no fear. Purely physical ties are broken by physical death. Nothing lasts but warm affection for souls on our own vibratory wavelength. Love of one soul for another is indestructible. Sometimes when friends meet after death, they may have to part for a little while for the newly arrived soul to go on with his training, but both know the separation is the best for them and are willing to work and wait.

On this plane, news of one's friends can be had from time to time, and we know all is well with them.

"The particular thing I want to speak about today is the suffering of the great Master Christ when He was living in the body of Jesus. All those three years He was exposed to trials and hardships of all kinds and very rarely did He leave the body of his faithful disciple, and then only for a short time.

"He left it finally on the night of the betrayal. Many people may wonder how such a mighty spirit as our Master Christ could possibly suffer. The great Master knew what it was to be cold and tired and hungry, where his physical body was concerned. All those discomforts were as nothing to what His Holy Spirit felt, when he saw how difficult it was to make anyone understand even a fraction of what He came to teach.

"All great teachers have had to go through that, and the very worst to bear is the utter loneliness of spirit and the feeling that it is impossible to get in touch with any other human soul. The Master drank that cup to the dregs and knew what travail of soul meant. His satisfaction came from His knowledge; it would all come out right in the end.

"Many people will dislike the idea of the Master withdrawing from the body of His faithful worker before the crucifixion. Do you know why he withdrew, Mother? His work was finished in that earthly body. There remained the final test for the disciple, Jesus of Nazareth. You remember the story of the agony in the garden? The disciple, Jesus, great soul that he was, nearly failed then, but our Master was with him all the time, helping him and putting all the spiritual force into him that was possible.

"The end of it, as you know, was that great death, that mighty unselfish death of the body on the cross and the gain to the disciple Jesus, and the immortal glory of being the first conscious martyr for the cause of righteousness on the earth. He had been training to that end all his life, and made the supreme sacrifice, consciously, gladly and uncomplainingly. "For this cause came I into the world."

These letters are excerpts from the book the witness now out of print. Jack and his mother are together on the other side of life. We never lose our own.

CHAPTER XV

PROTECTION AGAINST PSYCHIC FORCES

The movie "The Exorcist" created panic and fear in the minds of many people but it also brought the fact of psychic possession into awareness insofar as the public was concerned. The danger is a real one for some people. But it is not for others. For some, either fear or guilt is responsible for some of their troubles. If the little self (the subconscious) thinks someone on this plane, or on the next, has the power to hurt it, then that belief has all power. It is important to remember that we give people the only power they have over us. For instance, if we have an enemy and he finds a way to make us believe that he is going to attack us, particularly on the psychic level, we can easily believe that he has the power to hurt us. With this doubt planted in our minds, we become fearful because energy follows thought. The subconscious becomes more and more frightened because the conscious self is also frightened. One acts on the other like a chain reaction.

The fertile soil of the subconscious self has deeply implanted the *expectation* of evil as a result of the attack. Even if the pretender has no power, the belief that he has that power can cause us to believe it. Then the little self, who does not reason, may cause all the symptoms of illness or may cause accidents to happen. Then we say, "See. I told you I had a curse (or jinx) put on me. I knew it would happen."

It is the reaction to fear, and hardly at all to any actual power invested in anyone else, that causes the damage to us. Entertain a thought long enough and consistently enough, and soon the thought thinks you. This can work positively as well as negatively. For example, if you dwell on a virtue that you want to build into your character, and see yourself having it, you will. Correspondingly, if you dwell on fear, resentment or anger. these qualities will take you over. The remedy for fear of psychic forces is the same as that for the fear of the dark or the boogeyman of childhood. One talks to oneself and convinces the little self that there is nothing to fear but *fear itself*. If there have been any hurts done to others, one makes amends so that any guilt feelings that may cause the little self to feel it must be punished are cleared out. One builds up a picture of one's self as fearless, guiltless and fully protected by the High Self. This builds the thoughtforms that we send to the High Self in our prayers.

The affirmations and mantrams at the end of this book are good, for they are powerful, and if said with firmness and confidence, will be accepted by the little self. Repetition is necessary, for the little self is like a child. That is how the little self learns. Max Long gave a mantram to the Huna Researchers that was for those who had fear of negative forces:

"I refuse to accept any suggestion from any negative source. I merit only good and only good will come to me. I have the protection of my High Self about me at all times and it surrounds me with a robe of Light. I fear no evil. Nothing but good can touch my life in any way. I remained serene and safe and calm in the full knowledge that I am protected every moment, night and day."

For one who fears a cyclic attack or possession, it is wise to keep physically fit at all times. if the body is allowed to get too tired and run down, the normal charge of vitality (mana) may be lowered to the point where the conscious self is robbed of the power to control the little self, who can get out of hand.

The sign of danger is often the beginning of the reaction to one or more of the hidden complexes. There may develop a persecution complex in which everyone is seen as trying to injure the one affected. The fixations aimed at escape from the pressures of life may appear, where there may be fears which are entirely grounded in a complex and have no basis in reality. Many such fears are not recognized for what they are. A person who seems normal in every way may be convinced that some black force is at work on him and causing him endless trouble. The mental hospitals are filled with patients who are in the unbreakable grip of some fixed belief of this kind, or any of a dozen types.

There are psychic attacks by intruding entities from the other side of life, but it is not as often as may be supposed. One who is naturally psychic will have to be more on guard than one who is not a medium. If there is a tendency to be taken over, one can firmly refuse to be used. Max Long called these entities that get into the magnetic field of an individual "eating companions." Rightly so, for they use the vital force of the person they have invaded, in order to maintain themselves in the magnetic field. The person is tired and fatigued most of the time.

Some of my service has been in helping people who have psychic difficulties. It is well to know how to handle psychic forces before attempting to help the one who is possessed. If the helper is not full of vitality and protected by his High Self, the intruding entity can take possession of the helper. The intruder is not always an evil spirit. More often it is an ignorant one. It gets into the magnetic field of its victim and does not want to be sent on its own path of Light. In some cases, it has been with that person for years. My first case of this kind taught me so much, and perhaps my learning experience will help others.

Anna was a woman in her thirties who was psychic. I met her after I had bought a summer home in New Hampshire. She had heard of my interests and started coming to the house whenever she felt I was there. Anna was interested in psychic and occult matters and was an inveterate talker. She was not well balanced. I knew something was wrong with her. At first, I could not decide just what was the trouble. She insisted she was a reincarnation of her grandmother, her father's mother. The grandmother's name was Mary Flynn. It appeared that there had been great antagonism between Anna's mother and her mother-in-law, Mary Flynn. They hated each other. (Love and hate are the binding forces from life to life.) Anna said she remembered many incidents of her life as Mary Flynn. Anna's mother had a great deal of antagonism towards Anna and often made the remark, "You are just like Mary Flynn." The situation cleared for me one day when I asked her when Mary Flynn died. "When I was six years old." Then I knew. She was not a reincarnation of Mary Flynn. Mary was there in her magnetic field. To test it, I said:

"Anna, make the sign of the cross." We were sitting in my meditation room.

She stiffened and said, "I won't. I am not a Roman Catholic."

"You do not have to be. Make the sign of the cross."

"I can't. My arm is paralyzed."

There are two things that intruding forces fear more than anything else; the sign of the cross and the name of Jesus Christ. As I had to leave for Boston very shortly, I said no more. I knew I would see her the following weekend.

The following weekend I asked her to come into the chapel room with me, and asked another person to come in with us to act as a battery. It was a three-way conversation between Anna, Mary Flynn and myself. The conversation was as follows:

"Mary Flynn, what are you doing in Anna's magnetic field?"

"She needs me. She can't function without me."

"How long have you been there?"

"Since she was six years old."

"You know you have no business there and you will have to go."

Anna spoke up and said, "Who will I be if she goes?"

"You will be in charge of your own body and can live your own life."

Mary Flynn spoke up. "She does not know how to think for herself. I have done all her thinking for her."

I could see a smirk on her face as she said: "I told my daughter-in-law that I would make her pay for her nastiness to me, and I have. I was working through Anna when her mother would say, 'You are just like Mary Flynn.' My daughter in law did not know it was me. But it was!"

I could feel the satisfaction Mary Flynn felt because she knew she had given Anna's mother a hard time.

I was stern with Mary when I told her I was going to do an exorcism. I told her she would be banished from Anna's body and would have to go on her own path of Light. Anna pleaded, "Be kind to her."

Later, I was to realize something I did not recognize at the time. I could have sent her on her own path of Light with much more compassion than I used. Through the name and power of Jesus Christ I sent Mary on her own path of Light and Anna was free. But I wasn't, though I did not know it at the time.

During the following night, I awoke with my left arm swollen to twice its normal size and I was in severe pain. I received the impression it was a psychic attack and my reaction was, "Nonsense. No spirit can touch my body."

I was wrong, and it took me three days of pain before my common sense got the better of my stubbornness. I finally said to myself, "All right. If it is a psychic attack, you know what to do. Do it. What loss will it be if it is something else." I made the sign of the cross on the swollen arm and said, in the name and through the Power of Jesus Christ, leave my magnetic field, Mary Flynn, and go back to your

111

Source and be lifted up for Light." In fifteen minutes, my arm was back to normal.

In this first experience of this kind, I had made the mistake of not protecting myself ahead of time with Light and prayer. Never have I made the same mistake again. This experience left me with a feeling that returns to me quite often. How many physical ills may not be caused by physical problems. I had been so sure that a nonphysical entity could not attack my physical body. I was wrong. From that time on, I used the "Robe of Light" prayer that is in the last chapter of this book. Never has there been an invasion like this one again.

CHAPTER XVI

ASTROLOGY, ITS PLACE IN THE PLAN

Astrology's true purpose is to help us find our way out of dependence on external influences so we can be free souls guided only by the light of our own inner being. Our birth chart shows us where we are in our evolutionary progress. It shows what we have as equipment for our present journey. It shows the talents we have gathered in other lifetimes through experience. It also shows the weaknesses in our character that can cause us difficulties until they are overcome.

We do not come unbound into this livingness. The birth chart shows what we have to work out in the present lifetime. It shows what grade we are in as far as the planetary school is concerned. Astrology also deals with seasons, and the cycles of life. Everything on the earth plane manifests in cycles. There are right times for action as well as wrong times. If we plant tomatoes in December in New England, they do not grow. This is an example of wrong timing.

There are seasons in our mental and emotional vehicles as well as in nature. There is 'a time to sew and a time to reap.' Each cycle in our personal lives has its own meaning and its own purpose. Youth, maturity and old age are differing cycles. And understanding of the birth chart helps us to know what cycles are operating, and the right time to launch out into the mainstream of activity and when to wait until the cosmic tides change. There is "a time to be born in a time to die." In between birth and death, we have time which we can use wisely or waste that time through unwise actions. This is where astrology can be of help.

In order to calculate a birthchart the astrologer must know the date, year, place and time of birth. At the moment of the first breath the incoming entity draws into its magnetic field the energy patterns of that particular time and place. The energy flow in the magnetic field of the earth is synchronized with the energy pattern of the incoming soul. Just as the soul picks its parents before it comes down into matter, so it picks the time of its entrance into a physical body. Whether it is a so-called natural birth, a premature birth or a cesarean birth makes no difference. The doctor on the physical plane may think he has made the decision to induce birth. He has not. It is the soul which decides when the timing is right and is compatible with his appropriate pattern.

When given the right information a competent and dedicated astrologer can prove the validity of astrology. Astrology is not the nonsense printed in the daily newspapers. It is not fatalistic. The wise person can control the energies in his magnetic field and thereby rule his stars. Always the choice is there: to rule or be ruled. Like a skipper steering his boat on a vast ocean, he knows the tides and how to navigate the boat successfully; so the wise man learns to handle his energies and can use the cosmic tides effectively. This is what astrology is all about.

Having been an astrological consultant and teacher for almost 40 years, I can say from experience that astrology can be of aid in our ongoing. It shows where the road is smooth, and you can proceed without strain. It shows where the road will be rough, and it will be necessary to slow down, to proceed with caution and at a slow pace. It shows where the road is washed out, and you would be wise to take a detour. It shows when there are emotional storms coming up on the horizon. If squalls are coming up, it is smart to steer your lifeboat into a safe harbor to wait for the storm to pass. An understanding of the energies operating at that time keeps one from rushing into the storm. In everyday life if it is raining you put on a raincoat and take your umbrella and protect yourself against the storm. You do not resent the storm. The storms and beautiful days are all part of the living and learning process. This makes common sense, which among all the senses is the most uncommon one.

An understanding of astrology can be used to help man on his inner journey. When used in the right manner, it can be a tremendous help on his ongoing. A mini lesson in astrology may be of help. The planets are the energies that are operating, i.e., WHAT is operating. The signs that the planets are placed in show HOW the energies operate. The twelve houses show the areas of operation or the circumstances; WHERE the planets will operate.

When in astrologer talks of aspects in the birth chart, he is talking about the discordant or harmonious contacts between the planetary energies. These contacts show the wise use or abuse of energies in past lifetimes. If these energies are discordant in what are called mutable signs (Gemini, Virgo, Pisces and Sagittarius), they are faults that are just beginning to manifest, and can be changed by right thinking. If the energies are in cardinal signs (Aries, Cancer, Libra and Capricorn), they are faults of the last lifetime, and can be changed by constructive action. If the discordances are in fixed signs (Taurus, Leo, Scorpio and Aquarius) they can be difficult, for the entity has set up his personal will against the will of his High Self for many lifetimes, which creates problems that can only be solved by the person's relinquishment of his will. It must be a complete surrender.

A division of the signs that is very important is called the quadruplicities; the elements of Fire, Earth, Air and Water. These elements are present in all living matter. The amount of energy one has in these elements depends, not on the Sun sign, but how many planets there are in each element. The individual with many planets in Fire signs is spirited, full of zest and enthusiasm and has boundless energy. He is the bouncy type that is always ready to go. The Fire signs are Aries, Leo and Sagittarius. Taurus, Virgo and Capricorn are the Earth signs. These individuals are stolid, practical, materialistic and down-to-earth. They count success by how much money and how many possessions a person owns. The Water signs — Cancer, Scorpio and Pisces — are emotional and live their lives through their feelings. They are sympathetic, affectionate, moody and psychic. More important to them than material things, is affection. They want to be loved. Their lesson is to learn that you get it they must give it. The Air signs are Gemini, Libra and Aquarius. These types are the intellectuals, and everything must be perceived through their minds. These four faces of God are in everything in the universe.

These elements show where our energies are concentrated, for they relate to the four bodies through which we function. Fire relates to the spirit, Water to the emotional body, Air to the mind and Earth to the physical body. These are the components that make up the physical body.

Carl Jung, the European psychoanalyst, lists the elements as the four functions in every one of us. The Fire types are the Intuitives. The Earth signs relate to the Sensation types. The Water signs are the Feeling types. Jung postulates that we all have an inferior function and a superior one. He lists Thinking and Feeling as being opposites, and Intuition and Sensation as being opposites. Nature is always trying to create a balance, and these functions have to be brought into alignment. If one is intellectual, the ability to relate to feeling has to be brought into activity. The feeling types have to learn to use more of their mind stuff.

It is interesting to watch the different types operate. Imagine a group of people visiting a home. They are in the living room. the sensation type could tell you all about the furniture in the room and its probable cost. If it was expensive, he would consider the person successful. The intuitive would not be interested in the furniture. His interest would be in the persons there and what type of persons they were. He could intuit this very readily. The feeling type (water) would feel the vibrations in the house. Later, if you would ask him to describe the room, he would only have a vague idea of the surroundings. However, he could tell you if the house was a happy one or a sad one, and if the people in it were critical or loving in their attitudes. All of these temperaments are shown in the birthchart by how many planets each person has in the four elements. What a help knowing the birthchart could be to anyone in the counseling field.

There are twelve signs and ten planets. As evolution proceeds, the time will come when there will be twelve planets. There are seven planetary beings (they are called angels in Revelations), who are responsible for the evolution of the earth and its inhabitants. As the evolutionary process has proceeded, other great Beings were called from outer space to help step up the vibration of the planet. These agencies are called higher octaves. Pluto, planet of integration or disintegration, is the higher octave of Mars, which is action. Uranus, planet of intuition that comes from the Essential Self is the higher octave of Mercury, which is mind. Neptune, planet of divine compassion and sacrifice, is the higher octave of Venus, which is personal love.

As our planet revolves around the Sun in a yearly cycle, so our Sun revolves around another sun in a cosmic cycle of two 25,800 years. This is called the precession of the equinoxes. The movement of the vernal equinox goes backward along the ecliptic at the rate of about 30' every 2,150 years or 50 seconds every year. Just as the calendar year is divided into twelve months, so the cosmic year is divided into twelve cycles we call ages. At the present time, we have been leaving the Piscean age and entering the age of Aquarius. For each age there is a great teacher, representative from the Most High sent to earth and called the Avatar of that age. Moses was the Avatar of Taurean age. The bull is the symbol of the sign Taurus. The story in the Bible of Moses destroying the golden calf was symbolic of his breaking up the worship of the bull. The Mithric religion of that time worshipped the bull. After that age ended, the Arian age followed, and Abraham was the leader. Ares is symbolized by the ram and the lamb. The lamb became the symbol of the Messiah. The Old Testament is full of symbolism that deals with the Arian age. The Shepherd Kings — the Shepherd who watched over his flock — washed in the blood of the lamb — the Lord is my Shepherd — the Lamb of God slain from the beginning of the world — Ram in India the name for God, — Isaac sacrificing his son to please God and then putting a ram in his son's place; these are all symbols of the Aries dispensation.

We have been in the Pisces age for 2000 years. Pisces is a water sign and its ruler, Neptune, rules the ocean. The Avatar of the Piscean age was Jesus. All through the New Testament the symbols portrayed the age of Pisces. The disciples were fishermen – "I will make you fishers of men" — the loaves and fishes — the sign of Pisces was the symbol the Christians used to notify their followers where the secret meetings would be — the mitred hat of the Catholic Bishop is in the form of a fish; these were all symbols of the age. Baptism was with water.

Now the Aquarian age is coming in. The keyword of Aquarius is I KNOW. It is an Air sign and deals with the mind. To the faith of the Piscean age will be added knowledge. We will know why we have certain belief systems. The many therapy groups of all kinds springing up all over the country are teaching how to come to dominion over thoughts and feelings. These are Aquarian concepts being brought to human consciousness. It is a group conscious age. It will be the age of true brotherhood, but we are in the process of cleaning up all the evils of the past before true brotherhood can come. There is always the necessity to clear out the poisons before the body can be healthy. Until the evils come to the surface and are recognized, they cannot be transmuted. Every area of living — collectively and personally — is being challenged, and what is wrong is coming to light.

If this chapter arouses interest in learning more about astrology and studying it further, there is a textbook, "Astrology, a Cosmic Science" co- authored by the author of this book.[1] I say co-authored, for nothing creative or worthwhile is done by one's self alone. Without the aid of Higher Forces, we do nothing of great value.

---

[1] *Publisher's Note by Amy Shapiro:* In 1992, Isabel's text *"Astrology: A Cosmic Science"* was republished by CRCS in an expanded edition that included her book, *"Pluto/Minerva: The Choice is Yours."* At Helen Hickey's request, I oversaw it's editing. Helen and I later created: *"Your Cosmic Blueprint: A Seeker's Guide"* report based on the book. In 2012, I published Isabel's autobiography *"Never Mind"* in a joint effort with her grandson Jay Hickey — all available at NewAgeSages.com.

CHAPTER XVII

THE MAGIC SECRET — HUNA

Many years ago, I was privileged to come in contact with a teaching that was brought to this country by a man named Max Freedom Long. The teaching came from the Kahunas of Hawaii. It was the ancient Hawaiian magic that was known and practiced long before the Christian missionaries came to Hawaii. After that time, it went underground. Max long went to Hawaii as a schoolteacher. He, like so many of us, was on a search for the meaning of life. Although he had tried many creeds and orthodoxies, he had not found answers that were satisfactory to him. In Hawaii, Max long came in contact with Dr. William Tufts Brigham, who was a scientist and the curator at the Bishop Museum in Honolulu. At that time, Dr. Brigham was in his eighties. Dr. Brigham had investigated and studied the Kahuna magic that was known to the few remaining pure Hawaiians. The doctor had made contact with them and gained their confidence. They, in turn, gave him some of their knowledge and insights. Doctor Brigham and Max Long became partners in their search for the hidden wisdom of the Kahunas. Through Dr. Brigham's encouragement and Max's long arduous task of deciphering the ancient Hawaiian language, he found the secret of the Kahuna powers, and through the books he wrote, gave the teachings to the world.

His first book, "Rediscovering the Ancient Magic" (now out of print) was followed by "The Secret Search Behind Miracles." This book tells of his stay in Hawaii, his meeting with Dr. Brigham and his exploration of the Huna magic. Later he wrote "Secret Science at

Work." This book gives the technique of integrating the three selves, superconscious, subconscious, and conscious selves, as the Kahunas practiced it. What is exciting and meaningful is that it is a technique that anyone can practice for himself. Having taught it to others in group work and counseling for over twenty-five years and having seen it work miracles in the lives of many individuals, I can assure you, it works.

The Kahunas taught that we are a triune being and that we have three selves. The middle self, the conscious self, everyday reasoning, logical self, they call the *uhane*. The subconscious self was called the *unihipili*. Max called it the "*low*" self. I felt that denigrated it, so I have called it the *little* self. Each self has an etheric body and it is through this *aka* or etheric body that we get energy. The Kahunas called it mana, another name for vital force. The High Self or Superconscious Self they called the *Aumakua*. Each self has a part to play. Until we learn how to align these three selves and teach them to work together, there is no possibility of having the power to handle life successfully.

The middle self is the everyday self and it is the reasoning logical self — or it should be! Its abode is in the head. The little self is tied with our emotions and feelings, and its abode is in the region of the solar plexus. It is the 'gut' feelings we have. when we have taught it to love, and to know it is loved, it resides in the heart.

The subconscious does not reason. It is highly suggestible and accepts any thoughts or ideas the conscious self gives it. Every suggestion given to it is accepted as truth. Many wrong thoughts and ideas planted there when we were children are still there long after the conscious mind has forgotten them. The subconscious self is the connecting link between the conscious self and the High Self. Until we have made a friend instead of an enemy of our little self, the power that lies in the High Self is unavailable to us.

In Max Long's book "Secret Science at Work," he suggests that we make a pendulum with a cord or string about 4 or 5 inches long, and attach a bauble, or something heavy and pointed, to weight it down. I used a prism at first, and then a small heart-shaped locket. My little self liked that locket better. Then I took an inverted saucer, put it on a piece of paper and made a circle, then I drew two lines inside: ⊕

I told my subby, whom I named Jimmy, that the horizontal line would mean "no" and the vertical line would stand for "yes." A counterclockwise swing of the pendulum would mean incorrect and a clockwise swing would mean correct. A horizontal line in this direction \ would mean "in doubt." With my voluntary muscles I showed my little self what the pendulum swing would signify. The involuntary muscles are in the charge of the subconscious self, and through the involuntary muscles he could answer me. After fifteen minutes he did, and we started to communicate with each other. I asked questions and found out how my subby felt about things.

The ability to gain the love and confidence of the little self is worth any effort we make. Give it a name, then ask if that is what it wants to be called. If it says, "No," ask it to swim up into your mind a name it wants to have. Think of it as a little child who lives inside of you in is about 8 years old. Each morning when you wake, say "Good morning, little self. I love you and God loves you and we are going to have a beautiful day." When it is time for sleep, thank it for all the help it has given you during the day. Assure that little self how much you love it, and how much God loves it too. In my counseling and teaching, I have found so many people who have no recognition of their own worth, accompanied by a deep feeling of inadequacy. Once they make conscious contact with their little selves and learn to love it, that feeling leaves. That relationship gives no sense of ego for the ego belongs to the conscious level. When they learn to love themselves properly, they can also love others rightly. What a difference it makes! They have taught their little selves that it is alright if they do not like certain people. They do not need to feel guilty about it. Liking is of the personality and has to be earned. But Love is the Essential Being in action and is always there and can work at any and all times. Once the little self really understands that God loves us, no matter what we do, it is not so difficult to love those we may not like.

The Kahuna's called the Aumakua the High Self, the Parental Spirit who watch is over the two selves down here. To them, the parental spirit was both father and mother — our cosmic parents. As we have an earthly father and mother, so we may have a cosmic father and mother. I have wondered if this is the meaning behind appointing a godfather and godmother when a child is christened. There is a beautiful poem in Max Long's book, "Growing into Light."

> Parental spirits whom I love
> And whom I know love me
> Come through the door I open wide,
> Reveal thyselves to me.

It is the contact with the High Self that is of vital importance to those of us who are on the earth plane. In that part of us lies all the wisdom we need, all the love we could ever radiate or receive, and all the power we need to achieve our goals and objectives. The one and only condition that is mandatory for the relationship with the High Self is HARMLESSNESS — NO HURT. If we have done any harm or hurt others (and we all have), then we must make amends in any way we can. If the person or persons are no longer where we can go and ask forgiveness, than some sacrifice (something that hurts) must be offered up in their name. Then the little self releases its guilt and knows the debt has been paid. Then it is no longer afraid to go to its Parental Spirit and ask for help.

Make your little self your best friend. Thank it daily for all it does for you. It handles all the body functions. We do not have to tell our hearts to beat or our lungs to breathe. It does a million things for us. Certainly, a "thank you" is in order! If we work 24 hours a day, seven days a week and never received any appreciation or recognition, how would we feel? Do you need a parking place when you go anywhere? Before you get there, tell your little self to take care of it. He will. Lost something? Ask your subby to find it. He will. Are you out of rhythm and all tensed up? Quiet down and ask your subby go to your High Self and bring back mana (energy) to put you back on the beam. He will. Do you need help with a relationship that is difficult? Ask your subby to go to the other person's subby, and together make a contact with the High Self of the other person and your High Self, and then ask that new understanding and harmony be given to both of you. It works without having to do anything about it in the world of appearance.

In the tarot cards there is a card that depicts the three selves. They Aumakua, the High Self, is portrayed as an angel above a man and a woman. The man represents the conscious self. He is looking at the woman, the receptive female who represents the subconscious self. She is looking at the High Self. Both are naked for truth needs no covering. This card is called The Lovers. And that's the way it is.

Wherever Max Freedom Long is in God's great Universe, we bless him and love him for what he did for so many of us in bringing the Kahuna magic into our lives. May it help you as it has helped us.

CHAPTER XVIII

EXPERIMENTS IN HUNA

In 1948, the Huna Research Associates were formed, and I became a member. Its goals and objectives were to see if the Huna magic would work in today's world. We were to take the techniques of the Kahunas and practice them and see if our lives would improve through their use. We were to find out if we could build a better future. As Max said, "We have to start and experiment." He told us to do what we could to handle our guilt complexes or fixations. We were to dwell daily on the Huna teaching that no act is a sin unless it hurts someone. We learned to communicate with our Little Selves asking questions constantly in order to find out how the Little Self felt about things. Max told us to explain to the Little Self that it may be holding ideas that needed to be explored. Some of the questions were:

Do you think we should be punished for past sins?

Is there something you fear?

Do you think we do not deserve to be prosperous? Happy? Healthy? Why do you think so?

Do you love me?

Do you feel I love you?

Get your "Subby" to tell you who it dislikes and why? Go slowly and make a careful beginning so it will not refuse to go along with the questioning. as the Little Self is not logical, do not be surprised at some of its answers. Show it that you are working together as dear friends and for mutual benefit. Keep a record of your time and communication without Little Self.

It is our High Self with whom we want to make contact an in order to do so the way through the Little Self has to be cleared. The High Self is powerless to act unless it is invited to do so. We must comply with the conditions that allow the High Self to operate. The two selves down here must learn by experience. This is the law. This is our God-given free will. If we recognize we have no wisdom here on this level and ask the High Self to guide and direct us (opening the door) there is great joy in the higher regions. If we ask the great company of High Selves to help the earth children, there is great rejoicing. This is the true salvation. To be worthy of the help of the Aumakuas, we must try to emulate them. We must be loving, not judgmental. We must be willing to help others unselfishly. We must learn to give and not to grab.

I found that the more I prayed for others and helped them, the more help I received for myself. Every blessing that flows through us to bless others blesses us. I learned that when I made a prayer, sending a surcharge of mana with it to the High Self, I was not to dictate to the High Self *how* things were to be brought into "manifestation." "He has a way I know not of, and His ways are higher than mine as the heavens are above the earth." How many times I reminded myself of this sentence so I would not try to play God.

One of the basic steps we learned in the Huna Research group was to acquire a surcharge of mana to send to the High Self with the request or prayer. The Little Self had to be instructed to make this vital force. The Little Self understands a physical action. I would rub my hands together and take some long slow breaths when I asked Jimmy (my "subby") to create a surcharge of mana. Then I would take my pendulum, asking Jimmy to swing it vigorously if he had done so. Sometimes I would say, "I am now filling my magnetic field with a very large extra charge of mana. It is flowing through me and into me like a flood of water. I can feel the flow. Thank you.

128

The Kahunas pictured this flow as water rising up within them and overflowing as water in a fountain. They breathed deeply and this acted as a stimulus to the Little Self. More breath creates more heat and energy. If anyone has congestion in the physical vehicle he can accumulate a surcharge of mana, placing hands over the part of the body that needs healing, and say "I am now feeling the accumulated energy (or mana) flowing into my body to heal, strengthen and make it perfect, as it was in my youth. Thank you, Little Self, for your help in doing this." Relax and wait. The release will come.

Plants and animals can be treated the same way. Every living thing responds to love and healing force. Enclosed in a letter I received from Max Long was a picture of himself standing between two plants. One was as high as his knees and the other as high as his waist. In the letter he said he had dug two holes when he planted them and put them both in at the same time. Knowing I was an astrologer, he wrote "What of your astrology and planetary influences now?" My answer was "You blessed and prayed for one plant, asking for the help of your Aumakua. The other one you ignored and left to struggle along by itself. You have proven when I have taught from my beginning as an astrologer. Go beyond the personality to the High Self and you can change anything in the horoscope. Without calling on higher forces you must struggle along on your own." A short time later a card came from Max saying, "Right on."

When we send a large amount of strong earthy mana to the High Self, it is able to use that energy to project what we want into the world of manifestation — the physical world. The one precept that cannot be ignored is that the expression must bring no harm to anyone. The Kahunas were logical as well as practical. They knew the present was not the future and that the time element on the physical plane was important. Our subconscious selves know that if we have a pain, we have it. If we say we do not have it, the subby grins and shakes his head. But if we say, "It is now nine o'clock and in half an hour this pain is going to be gone; I am rubbing it now to help get rid of it," it will go. The Little Self is impressed by a physical action and cooperates. It is prone to accept any suggestion which is tied in with physical acts and realities. Time impresses the Little Self. Many times, as we go to sleep, we can give ourselves in order to wake up at a certain time, and it obeys the command. When I have faith that my Little Self can do things that faith (feeling) is shared by that invisible helper.

The Little Self works through feeling or emotion. The desire or prayer that lacks the element of emotion is of new no use. This is extremely important. The Middle Self cannot create emotion by itself. When the prayer action is decided on, say it three times, feeling the joy you will feel when it is realized, and then say, "The prayer is ended. It now takes its flight." The Little Self learns by repetition and it helps to repeat the prayer more than once. In using the Huna technique in healing, I found this to be so.

There was a friend of mine who had been laid up for three weeks, with a bad back. She asked if I would help her to get a healing. I became quiet and asked my Little Self to go to the High Self and find out what was causing the trouble. The impression that came back surprised me. "Her subconscious self wants to punish her for it feels it is not being considered or loved enough." I called her on the telephone and told her that she was to spend the day loving her Little Self, and that every hour on the hour my Subby would go to the High Self and take her Subby along and asked for a healing. By six o'clock that night she was completely well.

Read the books Max Freedom Long has written and do your own experimenting. Life will be as different for you as it has been for me. You will never be alone again, for your Aumakua and your Little Self (unihipile in Hawaiian) walks with you all the journey long.

The Kahunas could heal physical conditions that no medical doctor could approximate. In "Secret Search Behind Miracles," many stories are told of their healing and hurting powers. They had the power to invest a stick with enough force so that when thrown at an enemy, the stick would knock him unconscious. The same fire that can warm a house can burn it down. It is the use of energy vital force that determines whether it is constructive or destructive.

The Kahunas knew there was black magic as well as white magic and some there were that used it destructively. In one of Max's books he tells of the way some of the Kahunas would kill their enemies by praying the death prayer. Their enemies would die by paralysis that started at their toes and would creep up through the body until it reached the heart. Then the person would die. Some years ago, I was giving a talk at a Lions Club in a suburb outside Boston. After the talk, there was a question period. To my surprise, a man asked me if I had ever heard of the death prayer. He was equally astonished when I said I had. This is the story he told.

"In the second World War, I was a Medic in Borneo. Some of our men had something the matter with them, which we were unable to diagnose. Paralysis started with their feet. When it reached their hearts, they would die. Nothing we did saved them. One day, I met an old native and told him of the difficulties we were having, thinking he may know of some tropical disease of which we had been unaware. He said: "There is a tribe over on the far hill which is working with the Japanese soldiers. They are praying the death prayer over your soldiers." He explained what the death prayer was. While I had my doubts that the man was sane, I asked, "How can we stop them?"

"Go over to that hill and capture some of them. Put them in the stockade. Tell them when the next GI dies, you will cut off their arms and legs, and they will die. They believe they cannot go to what you call Heaven if they are mutilated."

We went over there and did what the native told us to do. We captured ten of them and put them into the stockade. Not another soldier died of paralysis while we were on the island. At war's end when the GI's had gone, the natives were allowed to go back to their tribe."

I wondered if those who died were souls who had prayed the death prayer on others in former lives.

CHAPTER XIX

ALONG THE WAY

A letter from Thomas Hamblin, a spiritual giant in England, gave me much light. Long ago, he wrote to a troubled reader: "You will notice that I do not pray that the trouble will be removed in order that you have peace of mind. I pray that you may have peace of mind in spite of the trouble, and that you may enter into God's peace so that you do not care what happens or what becomes of you. When you have reached this point, I know all will be well with you in every way, and in the highest and best way of all."

If we could only realize that everything that happens to us has deep meaning. Everything we have disliked, evaded or failed to accept and to meet in the past (whether this life or a past one) returns to us again and again until the lesson is learned and is not needed again. We are born into families where we have debts to pay, adjustments to make and lessons to learn. We are faced with weaknesses that need to be strengthened, as well as lessons that need to be learned. If we accept these lessons, then we grow spiritually. We grow beyond blaming others for the way they treat us, beyond the disappointments, beyond the hurts. We try to fully understand and to change our reactions. When we know in our hearts, rather than in our heads, that everything that happens to us is something we have also done to others, our reactions will be completely different, and then we are set free.

Not long ago, I was in a bookshop and was directed from within to buy a paperback book titled "Many Mansions" by Gina Cerminara. It is a book on reincarnation taken from the Edgar Cayce's readings. It is a book I read long ago. I found it most enlightening and enjoyable, and I wondered why I needed to read it again. I took it home and opened the book at random and my eyes fell on this paragraph on Page 102. Edgar Cayce talking —

"The entity has often been disappointed in others. Know that first rule, a law that is eternal. The seed sown must one day be reaped. You disappointed others. Today, from your own disappointments, you must learn patience, the most beautiful of virtues and the least understood."

I had read that before with my mind. Now I heard it in my heart, for I had been asking in meditation why so many disappointments were the lot of so many of us on earth.

It was Thomas Hamblin who provided me with this mantram for times of crisis and problems. In trouble times I have said it over and over inside myself. "God is in the Center of this experience, and God is Love." May it help you as it has helped me.

Patience has not been one of my virtues. It is something I have had to learn in this lifetime. My teacher gave me a sentence to meditate on which I have never forgotten. "Patience is dwelling *understandingly* in the Now with a vision of the Plan."

We all have days when we awake, get up and face a day when everything seems to go wrong. Nothing, but nothing, goes right. The emotional weather is like a squall that seems to come from out of nowhere. Some time ago I was having one of those days. All of the things I had to do seemed to be too much, and I did not see how I could do all of the tasks facing me. I turned to my Essential Self — the self that stays upstairs and helps only when you ask for help — and asked what was wrong. The answer came swiftly on the ESP level.

"You are out of rhythm."

"Why?"

"Because you have become impatient and impatience is the grandchild of anger. Tune in for rhythm. Still the turbulent waters of your mind and everything will fall into place."

I took the advice, and obeyed. It was not only a peaceful day but exceedingly productive. Once more I was given the lesson that consciousness is the only reality. Peace within means peace without. When we become tense and nervous, it causes our outside self to respond in the same way. That is the time to tune up our motors and let the Real Self direct our lives and 'run the show.'

****

Sometimes we have to lose all that we hold dear before the self-will be represented by "I want" and "I will" are starved into submission. As long as our life energy is the blind animal energy born of the waters of feeling and desire, and the will is blind willfulness, they must run their course. Willfulness is the opposite of willingness. It obtains its energy from the satisfaction of its personal needs rather than from that truer sense of joy that comes in serving the needs of others.

One inturning, spends itself in serving others; the other, reversing its goal, increases as it gives out of its whole being in its eagerness to see others attain the freedom and happiness such as it has found.

****

In the new age we're going to learn not to draw our loved ones back to earth through grieving for them. It is selfish not to allow them to adjust to their new dimension. We are with them while we sleep. One of the ways you can tell that you have really seen them is that you will always see them young and vital. There is no age over there. As you go to sleep, ask that you may see them and that you may remember the experience when you wake in the morning.

Between 1875 and 1930 some of the greatest mediums the world has ever known came to earth to prove the continuity of consciousness.

135

The forces of Light knew what lay ahead because of man's inhumanity to man. They saw the wars coming in and knew bodies would be sacrificed due to greed and a desire for power. One of the great mediums, who suffered all kinds of ridicule and persecution, was Marjorie Crandon, who was the wife of a Boston physician. She held seances for scientists, the psychic researchers and investigators. She made no charge for her services. She would go into deep trance, and her vehicle would be taken over by a spirit on the other side of life. The spirit was her brother, Walter, who while he was in his physical body, worked as a brakeman on the railroad.

A scientist from M.I.T. named Frank Sherbourne told me about the seances that he attended. He said that the first time he went to the séance, he went because of pure curiosity. He did not believe the experience would be anything but a hoax. The group was sitting in a circle in a very dim light when they heard someone whistling and steps on the stairs. The door opened. No physical being was there, but a cheery voice said, "Hello everybody." Mr. Sherbourne said he felt his hair rising on his head. This was the conversation he related:

"My name is Walter. I am just as alive as you are! Why are you frightened?"

"I can't see you." replied one of the persons in the circle.

"Well, if you knew how to tune your inner dial to my wavelength, just as you turn the dials on your radio, you would see me."

"But where are you?" queried another person.

"Right here. Where do you think the next dimension is? It is all around you. On the earth plane, you folks say two things cannot occupy the same place at the same time. On this plane it can be done due to the differing wavelengths. At this moment, Sir, your feet are sitting in the middle of an engine I am working on in my laboratory. Your feet are not hurting my engine, and my engine is not hurting your feet!"

Mr. Sherbourne was also at the seance the night Houdini was present. Houdini asked to check everything over before the seance started. Marjorie acquiesced. After she went into deep trance, Walter came in and he was a very different Walter from his usual self. He was furious. He let out a string of oaths, and he called Houdini unmentionable names. He said there would be no seance that night because Houdini, their guest, had planted a file in the box to be used in the experiment that they were going to do that evening. He angrily declared that the guest had done this trick to discredit his sister. The door slammed, and Walter was gone. There was no science that night.

Perhaps one of the most exciting and astounding experiments was the one with the three wooden rings. Walter told the group they should get three wooden rings with no break in them. They should send one to the New York Psychical Society, one to the British Psychical Society, and keep the third one in Boston. He promised that on a certain night, he would bring all three rings together in Boston. Three different couples told me the story of the happenings on that evening. The lights were off. Everyone present was sitting in a circle. One couple told me that suddenly it seemed as though the roof had blown off and that a high wind had carried it away. There was a resounding bang on the table. Walter's voice said, "There they are. I am going. Turn on the lights." Someone obeyed and there were the three rings on the table in the middle of the room, tied together with no break between them. The group telephone New York and asked if the ring that had been sent there was still there. It was gone. A response to their cable to London disclosed the ring was there was gone. It is hard for us to appreciate the persecution and the difficulties that the good mediums had to undergo in the early part of this century. Marjorie Crandon was one of them. She held her seances an invited investigation so people would know the reality of life after death. Life IS and ALWAYS WILL BE.

****

Even in this modern day, there is little understanding of obsession among those in the medical field. If physicians understood the psychic world and knew how to deal with obsessing entities, many people in mental institutions would be released. There are entities on psychic levels who can invade the magnetic field of an individual living on the earth plane. Max Freedom Long called such entities "eating companions" because they sap the energy and vitality of the individual concerned. Obsession shows in the eyes. The eyes are the window of the soul. When someone other than the person in the body is looking through those windows, the eyes look strange and abnormal.

These entities get into the body in a number of ways. Sometimes it happens when a person uses a ouija board or engages an automatic writing. If a spirit can take over a hand or an arm, what is to stop it from taking over the rest of the vehicle? Sometimes entities take over when there is overuse of alcohol or drugs, which can weaken the protective shield that lies between the physical body and the next dimensional body. There are powerful techniques, mantrams and prayers that can help them when an entity tries to overtake a body. I have seen the effectiveness of these prayers many times. The name of Jesus Christ IS all powerful. Tracing the sign of the cross on the back of the neck of the individual can seal the magnetic field against any intrusion. The entrance to that magnetic field is at the nape of the neck.

Illustrations of actual experiences frequently enable others to help, so I share this one. One Sunday morning at an outdoor meeting at a Vedanta service in Cohasset, the girl sitting beside me started to have an epileptic attack. Very quickly, I put my hand up to the back of her neck. As I made the sign of the cross on that area, I said inwardly: "In the name and through the power of Jesus Christ, I seal your magnetic field against any intruding forces, and bring down the healing power of God."

Then I addressed the invading entity:

"Go back to your source and be lifted up for Light." Immediately, the young lady was all right. A physician in the audience, responding to her attack, returned to his seat upon seeing that the seizure had passed. After the service was over, a woman who had been sitting behind me came to me and asked:

"What did you do to that girl?"

I responded, "What makes you think I did anything?"

"I saw a living line of Light went down her spine," she replied.

Along time ago my teacher had told me that epilepsy is caused by an invading spirit who is trying to take over the body of an individual. There is a struggle between the person who owns the body and the one who is trying to take it over. I had been told how to help. This experience was the first time I had an opportunity to try the technique I had been taught. How satisfying and wonderful to find that it worked!

Another instance occurred with a young man of eighteen, named Ziegfield. He had been brought to this country as a refugee, by a man who had a very bad temper. Ziegfield had seen his parents killed by communists, and his sisters raped and taken away. I warned the gentleman that had brought him here to be very careful in his treatment of this boy. I felt strongly that any further shock could send the boy off the deep end. One morning the man became enraged over something trivial that the boy had done which displeased him. As he ranted and raved, Ziegfield slumped to the floor, unconscious. When he was brought back to consciousness, he was a blithering idiot with vacant eyes and a body shaking with tremors. The guardian telephoned me and pleaded for help.

Unfortunately, I was unable to respond immediately. Two days later I was able to do so. Before I left home, I had a meditation and asked for guidance. The impression I received was that the boy had been taken over by an obsessing spirit. Further, I was impressed to say the Lord's prayer silently, and put the cross on the back of his neck while saying the mantram inwardly. (Incidentally, this technique of making the sign of the cross is opposite to the way the Roman Catholic makes it. You make the sign horizontally first to cross out the negative influence. Then you make the vertical sign to bring down the power.) When I went into the bedroom, Ziegfeld was sitting up in bed. He looked pitiful and hardly recognizable. My heart ached to see him in that condition. In addition to the man who had telephoned, there was a nurse in the room.

I was in a quandary. How was I going to put my hands on the back of his neck without telling them why I wanted to do so? Guidance came and I knew what to do. Some years before this incident, I had been trained in massage, although I had never worked at it professionally. Addressing the nurse, I said: "I have been trained in massage and am a license masseuse. Would you please turn him on his stomach so I can massage his back? It might make him more comfortable." She complied. As I massaged his back, I said the Lord's Prayer inwardly. I could feel the struggle going on at the psychic level. I made the sign of the cross on the back of his neck, sealing his magnetic field against any intruding forces, and bringing down the healing power of God. Almost instantaneously, he turned his head and said in a perfectly normal voice, "Isabel, what are you doing here?" The man and the nurse were dumbfounded. It happened so suddenly. What they did not know was that I was surprised too. In half an hour, he was eating a big meal and was perfectly normal. He has never had trouble of this kind since.

I know these things are hard to believe. In the beginning they were difficult for me to accept. However, I have learned to accept these facts, for they have proved to be true. If the reader ever has a necessity

140

to use these techniques, do so willingly and confidently. You will find the truth for yourself.

****

It was at the end of World War II, and we had to move. The landlady's son was to be married, and he needed the apartment in which we were living. There were no apartments to rent anywhere. We were going to have to buy a house. We had no savings, but we knew our Heavenly Father owned the universe and that our every need would be supplied. We prayed about the situation and our prayers were answered. We found the house. We moved in and during our first meditation in the house, we dedicated the house to its rightful owner, our Heavenly Father. We told him to use it anyway he wished.

He did. For the first three years, I gave up my bedroom to others and slept in my studio in Boston. Others in need did come. The most temperamentally difficult person who came was an aunt in her late seventies. Her life had been frustrating and sterile. She had spent her lifetime caring for her parents, who lived to be in their nineties. She had never been married or known any life of her own. She was morose and filled with unspoken resentment. (Later she died of cancer.) We tried everything to make her happy. Nothing worked. It was like having a gray, soggy blanket hanging in the middle of the house.

One day I sat down in meditation and asked my High Self why we were unable to reach her and change her. Inside my head I heard a sweet voice saying, "She is the Pearl in your oyster." That puzzled me. Later, I telephoned a friend and asked her, "How are pearls made?" She answered, "A foreign substance gets inside an oyster shell and, in order to protect itself against the irritation, the oyster surrounds it with a pearly substance."

Then I understood. Our irritation could be the source of great beauty and value. We had been doing all we could to make my aunt feel loved and happy. She could accept or reject our actions and efforts. That was her privilege. We were gaining a pearl of great price in doing what we were doing.

We all have times when irritations get under our skins. If we so choose we can make pearls out of such irritations. When anyone in our spiritual family is having trouble due to irritations because of other people, we remind ourselves – "Oh, she (or he) is the Pearl in your oyster." We laugh about the matter, and its tensions are eased.

****

Humor is the greatest balance wheel in the universe. Long ago, some inspirational writing came through a disciple who wrote: "I am the Lord of Humor. From another universe do I come. If the children of earth would invoke me and use me, life on your planet would be much happier. I am a great force for balance, and that is why I come. Learn to laugh and let the joy that is your inherent birthright be loosed. Remember — nothing lasts forever, and nothing lasts for long. Take heart and rejoice."

****

A letter that has teaching for all of us follows:

Dear Isabel,

For the last two years I have been working full time and going to college at night. For three years I have been going to your group meditations. Although God and meditation nights have always been number one priorities, my pursuit of a higher education took much time and energy: so much so that I excluded people from my life in order to achieve my spiritual and intellectual ideals. A week ago I had a physical and mental breakdown. For eight days, I went without any sleep whatsoever. I was incoherent but I thought I was going through hell to get to heaven and would be reborn spiritually. I was brought to the hospital and was heavily sedated. After three days I figured out the breakdown was caused by too much studying. It was a real shock to find out that the brain does have limitations.

After you came to visit me, I knew everything would be well with me soon. I would like to thank you and the healing group for your prayers. I honestly believe that out of every bad experience something good happens. For the first time in my life I have now felt love. Even though I have cut myself off from people in order to study and meditate I have been overwhelmed by the visitors, cards, flowers, concern and love that have come from so many people. After hiding in my books for two years I have found people again. It took a breakdown to do it. God was showing me something. No matter how much we sit around and meditate on Love and Light and the compassion of God in Christ, if you cut off people you cut off God. Now I am looking forward to a more balanced life, a more moderate school program and an increased amount of people interaction. Instead of sitting alone in an empty apartment I am going to have more of God in my heart and have a good time again with the beautiful people that surround me. When I received the flowers from you and the group with a card that said, "We love you" I sobbed for half an hour because I felt pure joy.

God gave me sort of a spiritual rebirth. Because of my having the breakdown He was telling me that I forgot people, and in doing this I was not utilizing the God in myself to its fullest potential. For the first time in my life I feel such a tremendous love for people. And, I feel that love in return.

Helping people to get in contact with the God in themselves and around them is the most important thing on earth. Thank you for helping me and others to find God.

All of us are part of God. I thank God for giving me a mental breakdown from too much brain study. I know I will never have a breakdown from too much love. Love has no limits. Love always, Carol.

****

A spiritual sister said something the other day that gave me food for thought. She said that some souls were like unhatched chickens that had to be put in a warm sheltered atmosphere before the chicken inside could hatch. Cold disapproval would never give it the necessary warmth during the germinating time. Only love, care and concern would give it the right nourishment. The chick must break free of its shell (self) by its own efforts. If we try to crack the shell too soon, we would destroy the chick. When it has cracked its own shell (because it has outgrown it) we can help it, but the initial impulse has to come from the chicken inside the shell. It has to feel crowded, cabined and confined before the desire to be free comes. By bursting its shell, the chick is free to live in a larger world.

CHAPTER XX

PRAYERS AND MANTRAMS THAT HAVE HELPED

"I CLOTHE MYSELF WITH A ROBE OF LIGHT COMPOSED OF THE LOVE, POWER AND WISDOM OF GOD. NOT ONLY FOR MY OWN PROTECTION, BUT SO THAT ALL WHO SEE IT OR COME IN CONTACT WITH IT WILL BE DRAWN TO GOD AND HEALED."

* * * * * * * * * *

This is a mantram that many of us have used through the years. It has great power and is extremely protective. Over the years, it has been given to hundreds of people. Many of them, in moments of crisis, have proved its protectiveness. If you memorize it, visualize it and use it, you too will find it extremely valuable. In the earlier days, I had a client whose psychiatrist husband worked with alcoholic patients. He was able to cure his patients but each time he did so, he took over the obsessing entities that were bothering his patient. As a result, he would go on a two to three week alcoholic "binge." At those times, he would physically abuse my client. I gave her the Robe of Light prayer and asked her to use it the next time he started to drink excessively. A short time later, he was drinking and came toward her to strike her. He was within two feet of her when he stopped, fell back, and said, "I can't touch you. You are all covered with Light." From that day on, he never tried to attack her physically again.

One night recently, a friend of a spiritual sister to whom I had given the Robe of Light prayer was on her way home. The girl lives in Harlem. As she was walking along a deserted street, a dope addict pulled her into an empty building. He raped her and then took out a knife and said, "I will have to kill you so you will not report me to the police." She was in a bad state of shock but remembered the Robe of Light prayer and thought, "Oh God, put your Robe of Light on me." Suddenly he dropped the knife and ran as fast as he could out of the building and down the street. In both these cases, these men were not in their conscious minds, so they could see the Light and it frightened them. In one case, it saved a life.

Many of us use this prayer every day, putting on our Robe of Light before we travel the highways or walk the streets of the city. We also circle our cars with Light. It works. Try it. You can prove the power of Light for yourself.

* * * * * * * * *

"OH LORD OF LIFE AND LOVE, REVEAL THYSELF TO ME. OPEN MY MIND, OH LORD OF LIFE, TO TRUTH THAT IS FOR ME. THY SERVANT, LORD, AM I. GRANT ME THY HEALING GRACE, I PRAY, AND AS I GO ABOUT MY WORK THIS DAY, GIVE ME THE POWER TO KNOW AND DO THY WILL, AND THROUGH THY PRESENCE AT MY SIDE, HEAL AND COMFORT THOSE I CONTACT AND THOSE FOR WHOM I PRAY."

I have always loved this prayer and use it constantly.

* * * * * * * * *

"MY HEAVENLY FATHER OWNS THE UNIVERSE AND EVERY NEED SHALL BE SUPPLIED."

The constant repetition of this mantram took me from lack and poverty to abundance on all levels. (Of course I shared it, for the law of circulation operates on all levels.) Energy follows thought. Invest a thought with feeling and it goes over the track to bring you back exactly what went from your consciousness.

146

* * * * * * * * * *

"GOD IS AT THE CENTER OF THIS EXPERIENCE AND GOD IS LOVE."

When there is crisis and sorrow, this mantram can be of the greatest help. When the storms and hurricanes of grief and sorrow assail us, this reminder helps. I have used it many times when going through a Gethsemane experience. This mantram has kept me centered. In every hurricane or tornado, there is perfect stillness at the center.

* * * * * * * * * *

"THERE IS ONLY GOD AND THERE IS ONLY GOOD."

When we cling to this truth and affirm it with all our Being, no dark force can stand against it. This conviction will root out any negative power and it will have to leave. I know the power of this mantram, for I have used it. The forces of darkness did flee.

* * * * * * * * * *

"COME OH LORD OF LIGHT AND BEAUTY AND DWELL IN THIS BODY OF FLESH, RADIATING ALL THE BEAUTY OF THY PERFECTION AND WHOLENESS, THAT THE FLESH MAY OUTPICTURE ALL THAT THOU ART WITHIN. EVEN SO, COME OH LORD JESUS."

Some of these mantrams and prayers were given by one of the great spiritual teachers and healers that lived on Boston. Her name was Jane Revere Burke. She had a healing group once a week. She taught us that we could build up our power to be used as channels of healing through our willingness to get self out of the way and use these mantrams daily. She was the one who gave us the Robe of Light prayer. That prayer is being used daily by people all over the United States. The steady and constant use of these mantrams have altered my character, changed my life and given me peace and sustainment.

* * * * * * * * *

"INFINITE SPIRIT, ETERNAL FATHER, OPEN THE WAY FOR OUR IMMEDIATE SUPPLY AND DEVELOPMENT. LET ALL THAT IS OURS BY DIVINE RIGHT NOW REACH US IN GREAT AVALANCHES OF ABUNDANCE, NOT ONLY FOR OUR PERSONAL DEVELOPMENT, BUT SO THAT WE MAY BE A THOUSAND TIMES MORE USEFUL TO THEE."

* * * * * * * * *

"AT THE GATEWAY OF THE NEWBORN DAY, WHICH HOLDS WITHIN ITS SEALED HOURS ORDERED RESPONSIBLY, I STAND AND SAY, 'LORD OF MY LIFE, HOW SHALL I MEET THE DUTIES OF THE DAY AND REMAIN DETACHED, MEET EVERY NEED AND YET BE FREE OF TIES AND BONDS?' AND GOD SAID: 'THE SUN SHINES AND VIVIFIES THE EARTH. LIVE LIKEWISE. GIVE BUT ASK NAUGHT."

* * * * * * * * *

THE NEW AGE PRAYER

From the point of Light within the Mind of God
Let Light stream forth into the minds of men.
Let Light descend on earth.

From the point of Love within the Heart of God
Let Love stream forth into the hearts of men.
Let Christ return to earth.

From the Center where the Will of God is known
Let purpose guide the little wills of men.
The Purpose which the Masters know and serve.

From the Center which we call the race of men
Let the Plan of Love and Light work out,
And may it seal the door where evil dwells.

Let Light and Love and Power restore the Plan on earth.
So let it be and help us to do our part.

This prayer is the invocating of the aid of the Forces of Light and is sent out daily by disciples everywhere. It has been translated into twenty-six languages. It can bring the light and love needed to save the planet from destruction. The forces of Light have to be invited to come in and help. They will not interfere with man's free will. The first verse invokes the Buddha, the Lord of Light. The second verse invokes the Christ, Lord of Love. The third verse invokes the planetary hierarchy whose center is on the etheric levels over Jerusalem. (The new Jerusalem that will not pass away.) The fourth verse deals with mankind and brings the power of Love and Light to earth. If enough people all over the planet will use this prayer, the planet will be lifted into the heaven it was meant to be.

CHAPTER XXI

ALLEGORY
"WHY"

I leaned from the low hung crescent moon and grasping the west pointing horn of it, looked down. Against the other horn reclined, motionless, a Shining One and looked at me, but I was unafraid. Below me the hills and valleys were thick with humans, and the moon swung low that I might see what they did.

"Who are they?" I asked the Shining One, for I was unafraid. And the Shining One made answer: "They are the Sons of God and the Daughters of God."

I looked again, and saw that they beat and trampled each other. Sometimes they seemed not to know that the fellow-creature they pushed from their path fell under their feet. But sometimes they looked as he fell and kicked him brutally.

And I said to the Shining One: "Are they ALL the Sons and Daughters of God?"

And the Shining One said: "ALL."

As I leaned and watched them, it grew clear to me that each was frantically seeking something, and that it was because they sought what they sought with such singleness of purpose that they were so inhuman to all who hindered them.

And I said to the Shining One: "What do they seek?"

And the Shining One made answer: "Happiness."

"Are they all seeking Happiness?"

"All."

"Have any of them found it?"

"None of those have found it."

"Do they ever think they have found it?"

"Sometimes they think they have found it."

My eyes filled, for at that moment I caught a glimpse of a woman with a babe at her breast, and I saw the babe torn from her and the woman cast into a deep pit by a man with his eyes fixed on a shining lump that he believed to be (or perchance to contain, I know not) Happiness.

And I turned to the Shining One, my eyes blinded.

"Will they ever find it?"

And He said: "They will find it."

"All of them?"

"All of them."

"Those who are trampled?"

"Those who are trampled."

"And those who trample?"

"And those who trample."

I looked again, a long time, at what they were doing on the hills and in the valleys, and again my eyes went blind with tears, and I sobbed out to the Shining One:

"Is it God's will, or the work of the Devil, that men seek Happiness?"

"It is God's will."

"And it looks so like the work of the devil!"

The Shining One smiled inscrutably.

"It does look like the work of the Devil."

When I had looked a little longer, I cried out, protesting: "Why has he put them down there to seek Happiness and to cause each other such immeasurable misery?"

Again the Shining One smiled inscrutably: "They are learning."

"What are they learning?"

"They are learning Life. And they are learning Love."

I said nothing. One man in the herd below held me breathless, fascinated. He walked proudly, and others ran and laid the bound, struggling bodies of living men before him that he might tread upon them and never touch foot to earth. But suddenly a whirlwind seized him and tore his purple from him and set him down, naked among strangers. And they fell upon him and maltreated him sorely.

I clapped my hands.

"Good! Good!" I cried, exultantly. "He got what he deserved."

Then I looked up suddenly, and saw again the inscrutable smile of the Shining One.

And the Shining One spoke quietly. "They all get what they deserve."

"And no worse?"

"And no worse."

"And no better?"

"How can there be any better? They deserve whatever shall teach them the true way to Happiness."

I was silenced.

And still the people went on seeking, and trampling each other, in their eagerness to find. And I perceived what I had not fully grasped before, that the whirlwind caught them up from time to time and set them down elsewhere to continue the Search.

And I said to the Shining One: "Does the whirlwind always set them down again on these hills an in these valleys?"

And the Shining One made answer: "Not always on these hills or in these valleys."

"Where then?"

"Look above you."

And I looked up. Above me stretched the Milky Way and gleamed the stars.

And I breathed "Oh" and fell silent, awed by what was given to me to comprehend.

Below me they still trampled each other.

And I asked the Shining One.

"But no matter where the Whirlwind sets them down, they go on seeking Happiness?"

"They go on seeking Happiness."

"And the Whirlwind makes no mistakes?"

"The Whirlwind makes no mistakes."

"It puts them sooner or later, where they will get what they deserve?"

"It puts them sooner or later when they will get what they deserve."

Then the load crushing my heart lightened, and I found I could look at the brutal cruelties that went on below me with pity for the cruel. And the longer I looked the stronger the compassion grew.

And I said to the Shining One:

"They act like men goaded."

"They are goaded."

"What goads them?"

"The name of the goad is Desire."

Then, when I had looked a little longer, I cried out passionately: "Desire is an evil thing."

But the face of the Shining One grew stern and his voice rang out, dismaying me.

"Desire is not an evil thing."

I trembled and thought withdrew herself into the innermost chamber of my heart. Till at last I said: "It is Desire that nerves men on to learn the lessons God has set."

"It is desire that nerves them."

"The lessons of Life and Love?"

"The lessons of Life and Love!"

Then I could no longer see that they were cruel. I could only see that they were learning. I watched them with deep love and compassion, as one by one the whirlwind carried them out of sight.

— Anonymous —

Made in the USA
Middletown, DE
21 December 2020

29681811R00104